PRIVILEGE AND CREATIVE DESTRUCTION

PRIVILEGE AND CREATIVE DESTRUCTION

The
Charles River Bridge
Case

STANLEY I. KUTLER

THE JOHNS HOPKINS UNIVERSITY PRESS
Baltimore and London

To My Father and Mother

Originally published by J. B. Lippincott Company in 1971 in a hardcover
edition. First published in a paperback edition in 1978 by W. W. Norton &
Company.

Johns Hopkins Paperbacks edition, 1990

The Johns Hopkins University Press
701 West 40th Street
Baltimore, Maryland 21211
The Johns Hopkins Press Ltd., London

Library of Congress Cataloging-in-Publication Data

Kutler, Stanley I.
Privilege and creative destruction : the Charles River Bridge case / Stanley
I. Kutler.
p. cm.
Originally published: Philadelphia : Lippincott, 1971.
Includes bibliographical references.
ISBN 0-8018-3983-1 (pbk.)
1. Charles River Bridge (Mass.)   2. Eminent domain—Massachusetts—
History.   I. Title.
[KF5541.C48K8   1990]
346.7304′4—dc20
[347.30644]
89-38367 CIP

"*The final cause of law is the welfare of society. The rule that misses its aim cannot permanently justify its existence.... Logic and history and custom have their place. We will shape the law to conform to them when we may; but only within bounds. The end which the law serves will dominate them all.*"

BENJAMIN N. CARDOZO,
The Nature of the Judicial Process (1921)

"*Fear, Craft and Avarice
Cannot rear a State.*"

RALPH WALDO EMERSON,
Politics (1844)

CONTENTS

PREFACE
TO THE 1990
EDITION

THE BITTER CONTEST over the Charles River bridges in the 1830s remains relevant as an example of law responding to technological and economic change, and political and social pressure demanding the assimilation of such change. The conflict over the competing old and new bridges spanning the Charles River was classic, pitting those who contended that property rights were inviolate against those who argued that the state might restrict such rights in behalf of the welfare of the entire community.

For more than a century and a half, the Charles River Bridge case has endured as a constitutional guide for resolving this fundamental question of public policy. Specifically, the case involved the necessity for compensation if government-sponsored activity impaired an existing property interest or form. The issue and its accompanying rhetoric have resonated throughout American history—in the Progressive Era, in the New Deal period, in the 1980s. We endlessly debate and attempt to balance the satisfaction of individual interest and the needs of the community. How, we often ask, is that public interest best served? Through unrestrained operation of market forces and unlimited financial rewards, or through some measure of regulation, scrutinizing entrepreneurial activities? The competing opinions of

Chief Justice Roger B. Taney and Justice Joseph Story in the Charles River Bridge case amplified the debate and reflected different approaches for weighing the common pursuit of individual interests against the larger rights of the public. The modern controversy over the use and control of the environment offers a particularly sharpened version of this ongoing struggle.

I am pleased with the opportunity to offer a new edition of this work. When written, twenty years ago, it marked an attempt to move beyond some of the traditional boundaries of "constitutional history" to what was then emerging as the "new legal history." Definitions of such concepts often are impractical, and certainly inadequate. For me, legal history dictates more than an exploration of the opinions of appellate courts. As such, I thought it useful to work backward from a significant decision, backward to the point of understanding the social, economic, cultural, and political conflicts that produced litigation and led to the judicial forum. Just as the biography of an individual illuminates the subject's times, so the "biography" of a case offers insight into societal concerns and conflicts over a focused issue. This book has afforded me many satisfactions, but perhaps none greater than the recognition that it provided (what one can only call) a "bridge" between the complementary modes of legal and constitutional history.

Republication also enables me to renew my gratitude to my long-time colleague and mentor, Willard Hurst, who, for more than a quarter-century, has stimulated and shaped my thinking about history. His theories obviously have informed much of this work. I also acknowledge again my debt to Joseph Schumpeter for his insights into the process of "creative destruction." I have found audiences in developing countries most receptive to his work and ideas. Yet the vagaries of interpretation of this valuable concept can be disquieting: recently, the *Wall Street Journal* applied the concept of creative destruction to justify the often mindless and irrational corporate acquisitions of the 1980s. The principle has enormous applicability; one need not stretch it to the point of absurdity to demonstrate its utility.

Finally, I rededicate this work to my mother and to the memory of my father—a mere token for all they gave.

PRIVILEGE AND CREATIVE DESTRUCTION

The Charles River Bridges: 1830

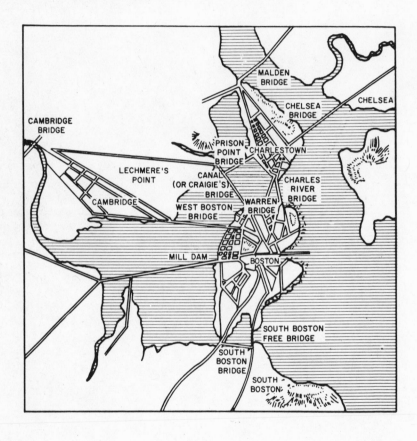

I

A TALE
OF
TWO BRIDGES

ON BUNKER HILL DAY, 1786, residents of Boston and Charlestown gathered to celebrate their new fortune. At last the two areas were linked by a bridge across the Charles River. Technical skills and entrepreneurial resources, encouraged by the state, had mastered formidable barriers to construct the span. While men had envisioned such a bridge for nearly a century, the costs and physical hazards always made it a risky proposition. But in 1785 the Massachusetts legislature granted a charter to a group of Charlestown businessmen who assumed the risks in exchange for a forty-year guarantee of tolls. With the bridge's completion a year later, the proprietors and townspeople alike could well congratulate themselves on their happy circumstance. There was a steady and sizeable flow of goods and persons between the two towns. In place of the old and unreliable ferry, and despite the tolls, communications now were faster and cheaper. And with the successful engineering feat, the proprietors knew that their bridge would continue to provide them with lucrative profits. Six years later the state extended the charter for another thirty years. The proprietors almost immediately realized their anticipated profits, and then some; by 1814, stock in the corporation sold for over

$2,000 per share, up more than 600 percent from the original price.

But in December 1828 there was new cause for rejoicing among some of the townspeople and businessmen, but certainly not among the proprietors and their friends. It was then that a second Charlestown bridge was completed. Overriding the proprietors' claims for exclusive privileges, the Massachusetts legislature had chartered the Warren Bridge Corporation in March 1828 to construct a new bridge nearly adjacent to the existing facility, terminating on the Charlestown side less than ninety yards from the Charles River Bridge. The new company could charge the same tolls as the old, but with a six-year time limit, after which its bridge was to revert to the Commonwealth and become a free avenue.

Constitutional rhetoric and considerations of public policy dominated the controversy over a new bridge. The advocates of a free bridge insisted that the state had never bartered away its right to charter competing franchises, and that the state retained the power to provide improvements for public necessities. In response, the proprietors argued that their charter guaranteed them a vested and exclusive right that could be abrogated only upon the payment of proper compensation. Constitutional principles aside, the antagonists pitched their battle lines around competing views of the state's public policy role. The proponents of a free bridge contended that charter rights should be strictly construed so that privilege would not hamper opportunity or the pressing needs of the community. The Charles River Bridge supporters maintained that the state must scrupulously respect existing titles and interpret their rights liberally in order to ensure a favorable investment climate for future private enterprises.

Defeated in the legislature, the proprietors turned to the courts in defense of their rights. First, in 1828, they sought an injunction from the state supreme court to prevent the completion of the bridge. Daniel Webster and Lemuel Shaw, their distinguished counsel, argued that the Charles River Bridge charter granted exclusive privileges to the corporation, and therefore the legislative act of 1828 impaired the obligation of the contract and was repugnant to the federal constitution. They further contended

rt. of state to override charter for public good vs. idea that it goes against public good to inviolate contracts that the chartering of a new bridge destroyed the tolls—in effect, the property—of the old structure and thus constituted the taking of private property for public use without compensation, in violation of the Massachusetts constitution. The court refused to grant the injunction, however, primarily because of the proprietors' ambiguous claims to exclusive rights. The state court subsequently heard the case on its merits, but in January 1830 dismissed the complainants' bill. The proprietors immediately appealed to the United States Supreme Court.

The Charles River Bridge case was first argued in Washington in 1831, with John Marshall presiding. Despite a determined effort by Justice Joseph Story to secure a judgment for the Charles River Bridge proprietors, the Supreme Court divided on the issue. Subsequent absences and vacancies prevented a decision by the Marshall Court before the Chief Justice's death in 1835. After the appointment of his successor, Roger B. Taney, and before a fully constituted bench, the case was reargued in January 1837. The Court's opinion followed the next month. A clear majority of the Court sustained the state's action and denied the appeal of the proprietors.* For Justice Story it was a sad occasion, symbolizing in his mind the evil days that had come upon the court and the law he revered. "With a pained heart, and subdued confidence," Story found himself almost alone as "the last of the old race of judges."

Such in outline was some of the rhetoric and passions of the Charles River Bridge case. The strident conflict of partisan, corporate, and governmental interests mixed the same elements of idealism and crassness that characterized the contemporaneous Bank War. There was talk, and much of it valid, of the "people" and of "community rights," yet what Massachusetts did in the noble name of "community rights" was unduly abrasive and largely insensitive to the rights of others within that community.

*Proprietors of the Charles River Bridge v. Proprietors of the Warren Bridge (11 Peters 420 [1837]). Hereafter see index for full case citations.

The legislature's charter for the original bridge in 1785, the free bridge controversy in the 1820s, and the subsequent judicial proceedings down to Story's closing dissent in 1837, might mark the bounds of the case. Within that period there is a rich story involving legislatures, courts, local politicians, and entrepreneurial rivalries. But the controversy always involved a large array of legal and public policy questions extending beyond concern for the Charles River bridges, in time as well as in purpose. Correspondingly, the triumphant principles transcended the case itself and have had a persistent vitality and relevance throughout American history.

Too often we tend to view Supreme Court decisions as if they were icebergs. The visible parts, the results, are readily perceived. And from this we recognize a "principle," which is either soon discarded or frozen into our legal fabric. But those results and principles are not abstractions divorced from underlying social and economic considerations. The Charles River Bridge case had much more at stake than a relatively petty local dispute over a new, free bridge. The Warren Bridge was a symbol for the rapid technological developments competing for public acceptance against existing, privileged property forms. The destruction of vested interest in favor of beneficial change reflected a creative process vital to ongoing development and progress. Within its contemporary setting, and for its historical significance, the case assumes greater meaning if railroads and the development of a new and improved transportation infrastructure — or even the benefits the community could derive from all inventions and scientific knowledge — are substituted for bridges. The competing principles of the parties in the bridge case fundamentally involved the state's role and power of encouraging or implementing innovations for the advantage of the community.

While there were alternative views of public policy at issue, the tension was more emotional than substantive. Both sides subscribed to a common goal of individual material rewards that in turn would benefit the community at large; the difference was one of means. A pervasive value of the age was the release of energy which regarded private property as a dynamic and not a static institution. An entrepreneurial rather than a *rentier* spirit was favored, and Taney's opinion was the quintessence of this preference. As the Chief Justice noted in the Charles River Bridge case, great and competing pecuniary interests were at stake and the choice between them had to be made with a practical legal doctrine. Moving beyond local interests squabbling over bridges, Taney posed the conflict as one between technological change and growth potentially beneficial to the community in general, and a private corporation's expectations of profits. In terms of public policy, the clash was between those who looked to the dynamic quality of law to release creative human energy and to stimulate economic growth, and those who emphasized the stability and order to be derived from a legal system that faithfully protected holdings and thereby created a constant and favorable environment for further investment. The advocates of a new bridge, and the court decisions that sustained their legislative triumph, were certainly not hostile to property; the difference boiled down to which view would best encourage investment—that key to prosperity, to that "public happiness," which so preoccupied market-oriented, bustling Americans.

More often than not, our law has been the product of events rather than of ideology; it has been utilitarian in both its developments and subsequent uses. External, social realities, not inner logic, have most shaped the law's evolution. Legal history, therefore, is most revealing when it encompasses the law's functional context and the interrelationship between law and society, rather than merely the abstract, embryonic growth of particular doctrines. The Charles River Bridge case, with all its ramifications, offers an opportunity for evaluating the role of law and legal institutions in accommodating the process of creative destruction wrought by technological and economic change. In a more general way, it offers an opportunity for observing law in its various settings—political, social, physical, and technological; and also as law-in-action, that is, in its derivations, its impact, its consequences, and the extent to which it furthers and fulfills society's goals.

II

FERRIES
AND BRIDGES,
1630-1823

THE PURITAN MIGRANTS who came to New England after 1629 settled north of the established Plymouth colony in an area ringing Massachusetts Bay. The more active and important communities developed around the estuary of the Charles River. They established agricultural villages both north and south of the river. To the south, they built Boston upon a peninsula slightly less than three miles long and a mile across at its widest point. Across the river, Charlestown emerged on a facing jut of land. Newton, later to become Cambridge and the seat of Harvard College, sprang up about two miles west of Charlestown along the marshy banks of the Charles. These river villages became centers for intracolonial trade and depots for foreign commerce. Bound together by common religious, cultural, social, and political ties, they were also mutually interdependent for purposes of trade. But despite their proximity to each other, the river presented a major communications barrier.

The governing body of the colony early recognized the problem. At a meeting in Boston on November 9, 1630, the Assistants ordered that whoever volunteered to set up a ferry between Boston and Charlestown could charge one pence per person,

and a like amount for every hundred pounds of goods transported. In June of the next year the Assistants reported that
"Edw. Converse hath undertaken to set up a ferry betwixte
Charlton & Boston," with charges of two pence for every single
passenger, and one pence per passenger when two or more
travelled. Although the ferry was private property, the Assistants
recognized that it was vested with a public interest. In 1641, for
example, they fined Converse ten shillings for neglecting his
ferry. Three years after the grant to Converse, the Assistants
approved a franchise to Richard Brown "to keep a ferry over
Charles river, against his house." They approved similar operations in the next few years, allowing different ferry concessions
on either side of the river from Charlestown, Boston, and Chelsea.

In 1640 the General Court, in a gesture of support for Harvard
College in Cambridge, granted the ferry rights between Boston
and Charlestown to the recently-founded school. Four years later
the magistrates and deputies of the General Court ordered free
passage for themselves. Since the grant had yielded little returns
during the seventeenth century, the college abandoned direct
operations in 1701 and leased the ferry to private operators. The
arrangement apparently provided that the college had to pay
maintenance costs, and records show that between 1775 and 1781
the ferry operated at a loss. At the end of the Revolutionary War,
in anticipation of revived commerce, the college spent £300 to
repair the ferry. It then received £200 annual rent, with good
prospects for clear profits in future years. But the ferry was
obviously inconvenient in an expanding metropolitan area. After
1781 the legislature required the ferry to maintain four boats,
but still the service remained inadequate. Therefore in 1785 the
state legislature, responding to pleas from Charlestown and other
communities north of the river, chartered a bridge.

The idea of a bridge over the Charles River dates back at least
to 1713. In April of that year Harvard College, alert to the potential threat to its interest, sent a delegation to the General
Court to protest a proposed bridge and to "represent and insist
upon the right which the College hath in and to the *profits* of the

said ferry." Several months later, the General Court directed a Dr. Clarke, who had applied for permission to build the bridge, along with a committee of the House, to confer with the college. It is not clear whether any negotiations took place, but nothing further came of the proposal at the time. Agitation and interest persisted, however. A pamphlet, published in 1720, entitled "The Distressed State of Boston," kept the idea alive: "[I]f there was a bridge built over Charles River, if £50,000 were expended to make it durable, and so a moderate toll laid on all carts, coaches, horses, and etc., this would help us by employing the poor, and the circulation of the bills would be of great service, and other things of this nature might be thought on." Boston town records of April 27, 1720 record an instruction to the town's representatives to promote the building of a bridge over the Charles River, "at the place where the ferry hath been usually kept,... and at no other place."

Massachusetts' involvement in the intercolonial wars of the eighteenth century diverted attention and investment capital from the proposed bridge. In addition, the technical factors offered a significant barrier — the depth of the water, the rapidity of the current, the treacherous ice floes in winter, and the distance to be traversed. Hence the scheme often was dismissed as visionary and impractical. In any event, these considerations deterred potential builders and investors for over sixty years.

Early in February 1785 a group led by Thomas Russell of Boston presented a petition to the legislature, requesting a charter to build a toll bridge at their own expense across the Charles River. Simultaneously, the legislature received a bridge proposal from John and Andrew Cabot, merchants in the town of Beverly. They proposed, however, to construct a bridge from Lechmere Point in Cambridge to Barton's Point in Boston. This was about one-half mile west of the ferry route. They asked for a "reasonable" toll that would expire after they were reimbursed for expenses and interest, with the bridge then reverting to the state.

The Russell group naturally received vigorous support from various Charlestown interests. The town's governing body submitted a petition to the legislature in behalf of Russell's proposal. The petition mentioned the suffering caused by the late war and how with common efforts Charlestown's citizens had "been led to hope for the pleasure of seeing their town arise from its ashes to its former state, and that with the blessings of liberty and peace, they might enjoy undisturbed the privileges of their ancestors, and transmit the same to their children." But, the petition complained, the town's trade and progress were hampered by inadequate means of travel and transportation, specifically citing the "inconveniences" of the ferry. While the petitioners argued that a bridge would be an invaluable remedy, they attacked the Cabots' proposal as useless and dangerous to Charlestown's interests, contending that a bridge from Cambridge to Boston would "occasion so great a shift of property" that the northern part of Boston and the town of Medford would be "essentially damaged to an amount beyond what will be easily conceived." Charlestown obviously had its own interests primarily in mind, but it skillfully tied these to the commercial center of Boston and its own hinterland, which it served as an entrepôt for trade with Boston.

A joint committee of the legislature approved the Russell application on February 25, 1785, and the full General Court confirmed the grant on March 9. There are no legislative records indicating a vote on the matter. It is likely, however, that the more numerous Charlestown area representatives from Middlesex County proved decisive in persuading the legislature to favor the Russell group. The combined population of Charlestown, Medford, and Malden then was approximately double that of the Cambridge area.

The preamble to the Act of 1785 declared that the erection of a bridge between Boston and Charlestown, "in the place where the ferry . . . is now kept," would be of "great public utility." The act incorporated Thomas Russell and his associates as the "Proprietors of the Charles River Bridge." The charter then set down certain details for the construction of the bridge, including a minimum width, the opening of the draw, and the number of lamps. It also offered an elaborate schedule of tolls, as follows:

Each foot passenger (or one person passing), two-thirds of a penny; one person and horse, two pence two-thirds of a penny; single horse cart or sled, or sley, four pence; wheelbarrows, hand-carts, and other vehicles capable of carrying like weight, one penny, one-third of a penny; single horse and chaise, or sulkey, eight pence; coaches, chariots, phaetons and curricles, one shilling each; all other wheel carriages or sleds drawn by more than one beast, six pence; meat cattle and horses passing the said bridge, exclusive of those rode or in carriages or teams, one penny, one-third of a penny; swine and sheep, four pence for each dozen, and at the same rate for a greater or less number; and in all cases the same toll shall be paid for all carriages and vehicles passing the said bridge, whether the same be loaded or not loaded; and to each team one man and no more shall be allowed as a driver to pass free from payment of toll, and in all cases double toll shall be paid on the Lord's day; and at all times when the toll gatherer shall not attend his duty the gate or gates shall be left open.

From these tolls, the proprietors were required to maintain the bridge. The legislature also provided that the proprietors were to pay £200 annually to Harvard College as reimbursement for the loss of its ferry. (There is no record of the college having interceded against the bridge proposal.) Finally, the bridge, in "good repair," was to revert to the state after forty years.

The Charles River Bridge charter offers a revealing commentary on the nature of public enterprises at the time. Many skeptics remained who doubted the feasibility of a bridge. Thus the burden of risk fell entirely upon the adventurers. If the project failed the loss was the proprietors alone. Furthermore, though no building or safety codes existed at the time, the state insisted upon certain conditions to guarantee the adequacy, adaptability, and safety of the bridge. For example, the charter required twenty lamps on each side of the bridge, kept well supplied with oil, and lighted in "due season" until midnight. The draw was to be lifted for all ships with toll, except for those passing for pleasure. The proprietors were allowed to take tolls to reimburse themselves for their investment, yet the state determined the exact amounts for all contingencies. Compare this to railroad regulations in the late nineteenth century, for example, which vaguely required that rates be "reasonable." For the bridge, the state decided in advance the matters of reasonable use charges and a reasonable compensation for the proprietors. The persistence of Puritan influence, with the obligation of the community to demand high standards of public morality, was still apparent in the provision for double tolls on Sunday. Finally, recent colonial experiences with monopolies, and an emerging commonwealth idea of positive government, combined to insure that the community would not be subjected to an "odious monopoly" in perpetuity.

That the legislature chose to grant a charter to the Russell group for purposes of profit, rather than to the Cabot brothers who proposed a schedule of tolls that merely would recoup their investment and development costs, raises obvious questions of economic ideology and legislative behavior. Beginning in 1792, and in recurring years afterward, critics of the Charles River Bridge company charged that the proprietors had gained their charter under fraudulent conditions, an allegation never proved. But what motivated the legislature to select the group that frankly sought a long-standing profit arrangement? There may have been some vague, but conscious, perception that the pursuit of profit, even at the public's expense, was a desirable good, one that would regularly attract further investments in behalf of the community. But, more practically, the legislature's decision probably stemmed from the intensive lobbying activities of the Charlestown community which was involved most directly, and whose need was clearly greater than that of its neighbors who would have benefitted most from the Cabots' proposal.

Originally there were eighty-seven stockholders in the Charles River Bridge enterprise. Besides Russell, they included such prominent individuals as Nathaniel Gorham, James Swan, and Eben Parsons, as well as John Hancock, who was now busily signing on for business rather than political ventures. Some of the Charlestown petition signers subscribed to the initial stock offering. There were 176 shares outstanding, but of the original investors only five owned more than three shares. Two of these held six shares, but Russell, Hancock, and Swan had twenty, thirteen, and ten respectively. Josiah Quincy later observed that an original share costing £100, or approximately $333, had returned the principal with interest and a profit of $7,000 by 1826.

Russell and Swan offer contrasting images of the character and style of the public speculator. Russell was an eminent Boston merchant with the touch of Midas. He was successful before the Revolution and afterwards pioneered in developing trade with Russian merchants. Russell prudently selected his investments and left a valuable estate upon his death. He participated extensively in community affairs, serving as a delegate to the Massachusetts convention for ratifying the federal constitution, as president of the Boston Chamber of Commerce, and as a member of the state legislature. Swan, born in Scotland, came to Boston as a clerk in 1765 and soon joined the Sons of Liberty. He participated in the Boston Tea Party and the Battle of Bunker Hill. He married a wealthy Boston woman in 1776 and became active in state politics. After the war he used his new-found wealth to speculate in loyalist properties and western lands. Apparently the Charles River Bridge was one of his few prudent investments, but he failed to enjoy its profits. By 1787 he was so heavily in debt that he moved to France, where he participated in a number of international financial operations, with only varying success. He went to a debtor's prison in Paris in 1808, and there he languished until his death twenty-two years later.

Construction of the bridge began almost immediately, and on June 17, 1786—the anniversary of the Battle of Bunker Hill—it was opened to public traffic. The bridge, built on seventy-five piers of oak, was 1470 feet long and 42 feet wide within the paling. It had six foot pedestrian passage-ways on either side, lighted by forty lamps. Major Samuel Sewall was the architect, and Lemuel Cox, "Master Workman," supervised the construction. The total cost was estimated at $50,000. The opening was a gala affair, attended by all leading public officials and by perhaps as many as twenty thousand citizens. One local newspaper reported that all were duly pleased with the event, but noted particularly that "those who know no other pleasure but the contemplation of their interest, were ... apparently anticipating the golden harvest which the immense numbers would afford, that either business or amusement will lead to improve this commodious inlet." Four days after the opening, bridge traffic, exclusive of foot passengers and cattle, included 20 coaches, 150 chaises, 137 carts, and 193 horses. The traffic undoubtedly contributed to increased trade within the area. For the proprietors it meant nearly £10 in tolls. The tangible community benefits were readily apparent. Before the bridge, commuters had to rely upon a ferry often inoperable because of violent storms or danger from ice. More dramatic was the reduction of the distance from the Middlesex back country. Wagons and carriages coming from Medford, for example, previously had to follow the river around through Cambridge, Brookline, and Roxbury to reach Boston, a distance of thirteen miles. The new span cut the line of travel to five miles. The bridge thus forged a vital link for integrating the area-wide market.

Success invites imitation, and other bridges flowed in its wake. Thomas Russell again led the way. Immediately following the opening of the Charlestown Bridge, he petitioned for a charter to build the Malden Bridge. Then in 1792 the legislature authorized the building of a bridge from western Boston to Cambridge. This project—the West Boston Bridge—immediately raised a protest from the Charles River Bridge proprietors. They complained to the legislature that a new bridge would cut their profits in half, causing "injustice and injury" to the bridge's stockholders. They contended that the original cost of their bridge, plus maintenance, amounted to nearly $80,000 in seven years, and that the new bridge would interfere with the retirement of that debt. The proprietors also suggested that the state's intrusion of unwarranted competition would "give a stab to all enterprise in the future founded on public grants; to add nothing on the advantages that have arisen from the bold and successful enterprise of your Petitioners, in raising other most useful bridges in this state." The state nevertheless authorized the West Boston Bridge.

But the Charles River Bridge proprietors did not entirely fail in their protest. The legislature conceded that the new bridge might diminish the revenues of the Charles River Bridge and therefore extended the term of the charter from forty to seventy years. The legislature backslid on morality, however: it abolished the Sunday double toll. Ironically, the 1792 extension of the charter planted the seeds for the future political and legal assault against the Charles River Bridge.

The proprietors' protest was based on a recognition that the new bridge would destroy their monopoly in transportation across the river. Until 1792 their bridge in effect connected all of Boston with the area north of the river, including both Charlestown and Cambridge. The new West Boston bridge provided for a direct route between one part of Boston and Cambridge and undoubtedly detoured traffic from the Charles River Bridge. It is unlikely that the latter's proprietors envisioned a permanent monopoly at that time. In their petition to the legislature they neither denied the state's power to create another bridge nor contended that the new bridge was illegal or violated any vested rights. Once the state gave them something—in the form of a charter extension—they came around. Equally important in the light of future developments was the state's assertion of its right to charter new bridges. Fifteen years later the state authorized the Canal Bridge, which was to be built halfway between the Charles River and West Boston Bridges. It followed the line of travel from northwest Boston to Lechmere's Point, near Cambridge, the same route proposed by John and Andrew Cabot in 1785. The legislature offered no further compensation to the Charles River Bridge proprietors at this time, and underscored the state's powers and prerogatives. A Senate committee found nothing in the bridge grants, "or in the principles of justice and equity," that could be interpreted as abridging the state's power to authorize other bridges. The legislature was free, it concluded, to charter any other improvements if they "would promote the convenience and accommodation of any portion of citizens, or advance the general interests of the commonwealth."

The Charles River Bridge owners did not challenge the Canal Bridge. They apparently acknowledged the legislature's right to act; and the success of their own enterprise was such that they could probably afford the luxury of acquiescence. The general level of prosperity and an expanding population brought the collection of tolls up to nearly $20,000 annually. By 1805 the stock shares of the bridge had risen over 300% in value; nine years later, Harvard College purchased two shares at $2,080 each. The population of Suffolk County, which included Boston and Chelsea, and of Middlesex County, containing such towns as Charlestown, Cambridge, Malden, and Medford, steadily grew in the years after 1790. Suffolk almost doubled its size from 1790 to 1810, going from nearly 19,000 persons to over 34,000. Middlesex's rate of growth, although less dramatic, was sizeable too, increasing more than 10,000 from the 1790 figure of 42,000. The tempo of growth accelerated even more after 1810. In the following two decades, Suffolk County added another 18,000 persons and Middlesex, 25,000. This growth proved a source both of gain and of sorrow for the Charles River Bridge proprietors. Bridge traffic naturally increased, adding to the coffers of the owners. But their very success spelled their doom. Although the bridge did not exclude competition, it still lent itself to charges of monopoly. With the increased trade in the area the tolls seemed more burdensome and obvious than earlier. The same tolls had prevailed since 1786, and the bridge owners' prosperity had increased almost in geometric fashion. In a day when opportunity was the watchword, and special privilege its bane, the proprietors appeared as keepers at the gate, extorting excessive tribute from those seeking their own enrichment.

The animus against privilege and monopoly was not a new phenomenon in American life. As early as 1641, the Massachusetts legislature had declared that "there shall be no monopolies granted or allowed amongst us — but of such new inventions that are profitable to the country — and that for a short time." In an expanding economy and society, such as that of the early nineteenth century, this attitude took on new vitality and purpose.

The assault on privilege provided the rhetorical rationalization for an alleged democratization of wealth. Material drives and desires seemingly possessed unprecedented momentum. Ralph Waldo Emerson in his Concord retreat found it all too apparent when he observed: "Public and private avarice make the air we breathe thick and fat." Almost as a necessary corollary, this passion gave voice to a clarion call throughout the land against established wealth, interests, and institutions. They stood, it was said, as a barrier against the "equal rights" of everyone to acquire wealth. But as Alexis de Tocqueville noted, the "love of property" disinclined Americans toward any levelling or confiscatory schemes. The American cure for the power of property was more property. Privilege and exclusiveness appeared as artificial contrivances that actually restricted, rather than promoted, material gain. David Henshaw, a young Massachusetts entrepreneur and political operator, typically justified the new materialism in democratic terms. Henshaw was an early and vigorous opponent of the Bank of the United States. He realized, of course, the desirability of creating new banks in its place, but he emphasized that stockholders of the old must not participate in the new. Naturally, he had his own designs on such a bank, but he carefully framed his argument in true egalitarian fashion: "The whole community should be offered the opportunity to have an interest in the institution on equal terms," he wrote. So spoke the new free enterprise, the new economic individualism.

Despite the popular currency of *laissez-faire* ideas, Americans really demanded a vital role for government. They regularly expected governmental intervention to encourage enterprise, and to remove the natural and artificial restraints on opportunity. Government, for example, deeply involved itself in transportation development and the regulation of finance and credit, its purpose being to enable private individuals as groups to engage their creative energies. Tocqueville observed that Americans primarily sought "for themselves a government which will allow them to acquire the things they covet and which will not debar them from the peaceful enjoyment of those possessions which they have already acquired." But this did not necessarily imply an inert government; indeed, as events of the 1830s illustrated, there was a tension, at times a contradiction, within this attitude toward government. Positive and abrasive governmental activity were sometimes necessary in order to satisfy fully the American acquisitive spirit. The Bank War and the Charles River Bridge controversy both showed that in the name of progress and democracy the government could destroy or seriously impair — if only by indirection — possessions persons had lawfully acquired. One individual could not despoil another's possessions, of course; in this sense, the right of property remained sacrosanct. But various property rights did not preclude the state from interfering with the uses to which property might be put when the state acted for the welfare of the entire community.

Americans perceived their government as a servant or tool, and not as some abstract and self-serving entity aloof from the concerns and needs of the community. Such an instrumentalist concept was useful in assaulting those entrenched privileges that barred community progress, and in eliminating or restraining lawfully vested private interests that inhibited newer and more aggressive entrepreneurs from realizing their full potential. In a time of explosive economic activity, prompted by a combination of technological improvements, expanding needs, the availability of investment capital, and an unyielding, and unquenchable acquisitive spirit, public policy had to serve the general welfare, not promote selfish gain harmful to society as a whole. In short, public policy responded to the calculus of the marketplace.

III

THE FREE BRIDGE
CONTROVERSY,
1823-1828

THE FIRST PORTENT of trouble for the Charles River Bridge proprietors came during the summer legislative session of 1823. A group of Charlestown merchants, led by John Skinner and Isaac Warren, presented a petition for a charter to build a toll-free bridge across the river. The proprietors protested, denying any need for a new bridge and calling attention to the threat posed to their property, then valued at nearly $300,000. There were also objections from wharf owners along the river who claimed that another bridge would further obstruct navigation. In January 1824, the Harvard Corporation expressed concern for its interest in the Charles River Bridge and directed the President and Treasurer of the College to make the necessary memorials and remonstrances to the legislature. Periodically, opponents of the new bridge scheme attributed it to Charlestown real estate speculators whose property would be enhanced in value by free communication with Boston.

Skinner's supporters introduced a bill in the legislature in 1824 authorizing a new bridge. No action was taken at the time, but the Charlestown group petitioned again the next year. The renewed pressure evoked a long public remonstrance by the Charles

River Bridge proprietors. They claimed that a new bridge would destroy property rights and involve severe consequences to related interests. They denounced the scheme as one designed only to relieve Charlestown's inhabitants from the foot toll. Obviously a new bridge into Charlestown was not going to facilitate trade with that city, or its hinterland. Discerning the motive for a new bridge, the proprietors indignantly derided the city's lack of gratitude. They recalled the inconveniences and "terrors" of the ferry and maintained that the bridge had brought untold prosperity to the community. They noted, too, the hazards and risks of their own investment, claiming that real estate investments would have been safer and more profitable.

The proprietors defended their interests by distinguishing frozen from liquid capital holdings. A bank, incorporated merely to use money, always retains control over its capital investment. But corporations created to build bridges surrender their capital forever. Once invested, it is irredeemable. There is nothing left but the franchise. The proprietors noted that in their own case the franchise included the right of toll, which was their only "property." Without it the bridge was worthless to them. Finally, the proprietors urged that the state adhere to "justice, equity, and good faith," rather than concern itself with "savings or gains" for a limited group.

The legislature failed to act in 1825 also. In the January 1826 session, a legislative joint committee considered the Skinner petition but it, too, recommended rejection. The petition was more elaborate this time, citing "public exigencies" requiring a new bridge. The petitioners contended that the draw of the Charles River Bridge obstructed travel; that the access avenues to the bridge were narrow, overcrowded, and dangerous; that a new bridge would equalize land prices in Charlestown and Boston; that it would serve the growing western part of Boston; that it would accommodate the naval base at Charlestown; and that it would benefit the users of the Middlesex Canal. Finally, to clinch their proposal, the petitioners charged that the tolls on the Charles River Bridge were "burdensome, vexatious, and odious." Naturally, the proprietors again protested. They denied that the legislature could rightfully grant the petitioners' request without compensation for the loss of tolls. This may have been a deliberate tactical move. The proprietors thus avoided giving an impression of being opposed to progress. They denied the necessity of a new bridge but indicated that they would accept one provided the legislature reimbursed their investment.

The legislative committee rejected the petitioners' arguments in almost every particular. The distance between Charlestown and Boston would not be appreciably lessened; the present bridge was "amply sufficient" to accommodate all travel, and there was no danger or difficulty in its use; land prices in either city would not change materially; and a new bridge would only further obstruct river navigation. The committee, however, suggested that the Charles River Bridge owners might construct an additional draw to keep travel flowing continuously. The proprietors themselves, in a previous protest, had volunteered to do so and periodically renewed the offer.

The committee's report stressed traditional views of property rights and public policy. Its major premise seemed to be that a new bridge would require compensation to the old. Merely to duplicate the facility and its services, in addition to the compensation costs, amounted to an unnecessary, if not intolerable, burden to the whole state. The committee had no doubts as to the proprietors' legal rights. It recognized that the bridge charter contained all the essentials of a contract, expressly granting the right to take tolls for a specified time. Citing John Marshall's decision in *Fletcher* v. *Peck* (1810), the committee held that the legislature had to execute the contract according to the original understanding.

The committee conceded the obvious advantages of a free bridge, but other variables figured in its social cost accounting. If there were a free bridge, the gain of one group (Charlestown's inhabitants) would be at the expense of others (the proprietors and the state). The legislative committee, as of 1826, refused to recognize any profit to the "whole community" in such a venture.

In other words, like John Marshall, the legislators considered the rights of bona fide investors, who had acted in good faith, as paramount. If their capital was insecure, the whole community would suffer for lack of investment and risk-taking in public improvements. Assuming the adequacy of the present bridges across the Charles, the committee also refused to impose the costs of maintaining a new bridge upon the whole community for the benefit of a few.

Finally, the committee offered an observation about "progress" that has a good deal of modern relevance. It noted that when a bridge or road is developed, people in the vicinity construct their buildings and generally adapt their business and pleasure arrangements to the line of travel. A discontinued bridge or road was, the committee said, "an evil of considerable magnitude." Such solicitude is probably unique within the American experience, and it is revealing that this attitude did not prevail in the bridge controversy. The construction of the interstate highway system in the 1960s offers valid comparison. The new roads often are constructed a few miles away from existing (and perhaps quite adequate) highways with fully developed services. For the sake of "convenience," new motels, restaurants, and service stations develop near the new road, and usually with financially disastrous results for the older businesses. What passes for enlightened public policy and progress is not without its brutal side-effects.

Despite the adverse committee report on the Skinner petition, the same 1826 legislative session produced positive action on a similar proposal. Two years earlier, David Henshaw, already an aggressive force in banking, sought legislative permission to build a free bridge from Sea Street in Boston to newly-developed lands in South Boston. Not coincidentally, to be sure, Henshaw and his associates had a heavy stake in the real estate. The South Boston Bridge, a toll bridge chartered in 1804, already provided an access from the point where Roxbury joined the Boston peninsula. The South Boston Bridge proprietors immediately opposed Henshaw's scheme with a protest to the legislature, claiming that the free bridge would violate their charter rights.

A pamphlet, published in 1825, and probably written by Henshaw, appealed to the "good sense" of the legislature and the community in favor of a new, free bridge. The pamphlet equated the "specious claims" of the inviolability of charter rights with the "spirit of monopoly" inherited from England, which still flourished despite the Revolution. Monopolies, it continued, thwarted the progress and general prosperity of the community. For example, after the legislature broke a statewide monopoly on banking in 1811 a dramatic increase of investment capital had occurred that materially aided the development of the state. The "light and intelligence of the age" dictated that the "interests of the many, and prosperity of the State, must not be sacrificed to the aggrandizement of the few." This antimonopoly rhetoric was thus a real article of faith long before the Bank War, which the Charles River Bridge controversy spotlighted: "To gain the road to improvement you must open the door to competition, and shut it against monopoly; the latter destroys, whilst the former nourishes improvement. The one benefits the few, at the expense of the many; the other benefits all at the expense of none."

Once the South Boston Bridge proprietors realized the force of the free bridge advocates' political appeal, they requested compensation for the diversion of their line of travel to South Boston. But the Henshaw group countered that the state could freely charter new corporations and need only reimburse for the property actually taken. The legislature granted the bridge charter to Henshaw and his associates in March 1826. It provided that the bridge was to be free and authorized state purchase after completion. Significantly, the South Boston Bridge proprietors received no compensation. Governor Levi Lincoln promptly signed the bill.

The legislature's authorization of the South Boston free bridge did not refute its simultaneous rationale against the proposal for a free bridge alongside the Charles River Bridge. Although the South Boston bridges terminated in the same place, the lines of travel were distinctly different. The eastern half of the Boston peninsula certainly gained a communications advantage as a result of the new route. However slight the impact, a physical need for a new bridge could certainly be justified more easily for South Boston than for the Charles River area. Yet the South Boston affair should have given the Charles River Bridge proprietors pause for thought since the vested rights and compensation arguments moved neither the legislature nor the governor.

Following the Joint Committee's report on the Skinner proposal, new petitions appeared later in 1826 and again the following year. The Charlestown petitioners still maintained that public convenience and necessity required a new bridge. The Charles River Bridge's raised draw and the narrow access streets impeded traffic. They also charged that the raised draw offered a hazard to Charlestown because it prevented fire engines passing from Boston. Once again the petitioners demanded relief from the "heavy tolls," contending that the proprietors had received an "ample and even exorbitant compensation" for their expenses and that further toll payments would be "a public injustice." Specifically, the petition from the town of Malden contended that the new bridge would benefit shippers of lumber and timber from the hinterland. These shippers transported materials on the Middlesex Canal to Charlestown, and then transferred them to wagons for shipment across the river. Presumably, this argument applied to all shippers using the canal who would have certain fixed transportation costs reduced by a free bridge to Boston.

The petitioners also interjected new issues. They claimed that the proprietors secured an extension of their charter in 1792 through fraud and misrepresentation of their financial state. They charged, too, that those burdened by the extension never had a chance to protest. Finally, they maintained that the legislature had an "equitable right" to interfere "indirectly" with the proprietors' interests by chartering a new bridge. They also noted precedents for such action, in which no compensation had been given.

The proprietors again denied any necessity for a new bridge, contending that the existing structure adequately handled the traffic flow. They acknowledged the problem of narrow accesses, but this, they said was a concern for the city governments. They noted moreover that street improvements often had been made at their own expense. They admitted that the draw caused certain difficulties, and to that end, offered to build a double draw, by means of a short circular bridge leading from the side of the main bridge, which would permit carriages to turn out from the existing draw and re-enter the main bridge beyond it. The proprietors also used the proposed legislation to expose the falsity of the petitioners' claims. The bill contained a provision that if the proprietors agreed within sixty days to relinquish their title to the state after December 31, 1831, the new bridge would not be constructed until after that date. Furthermore, there was no obligation to construct it at all. Nothing better illustrated the sham and hypocrisy of the arguments urging a new bridge on the grounds of "public necessity." The proprietors immediately drew attention to the proviso, claiming that it portrayed the true purpose of the bill — namely, to free the community from tolls.

The proprietors indignantly refuted the charge of fraud in connection with the 1792 charter extension. They found it remarkable that more than thirty years had passed for the wrong-doing to be uncovered. The allegation of fraud proved only a temporary diversion. Once the owners produced overwhelming evidence corroborating the financial state of the corporation in 1792, and the relevant legislative history surrounding the extension, the free bridge advocates for the most part dropped the charge. Still, it recurred occasionally, usually in connection with a discussion of the company's excessive profits, which further stigmatized the bridge as something sinister.

In 1827, the proprietors realized the futility of debating their opponents on the need for a new bridge. They recognized the emotional appeal of a toll free bridge and their response now assumed a new urgency. In addition, they weighted it with elaborate constitutional arguments, apparently designed to convince legislators and public alike that the proprietors' rights were just and legally impregnable.

The proprietors reminded the legislature that the state itself

not question of new bridge as much as toll-free bridge

had created the "public inconvenience" of tolls. If burdensome, then some adjustments were in order. But if they were to be abolished outright, "common honesty" required the state to make some indemnity. Again the proprietors insisted that the right to collect tolls was the essence of the contract between themselves and the state. Abolition of the tolls would thus constitute an impairment of the state's contractual obligations in violation of the federal constitution. Quoting European authorities, as well as William Blackstone and New York's Chancellor James Kent, they warned that the state could not do indirectly what it was forbidden to do directly. That is, the state could not erect a free bridge alongside their own, precisely because it would destroy any prospect of future tolls. Besides the requirements of the federal constitution, the proprietors invoked certain clauses of the Bill of Rights of the Massachusetts Constitution. First, they cited the guarantee that every individual had a right to be protected in "the enjoyment of his life, liberty, and property." The other involved the principle of eminent domain: "whenever the public exigencies require, that the property of any individual should be appropriated to public uses, he shall receive a reasonable compensation therefor." The proprietors described compensation as the great preserving principle of American government. It secured every advantage to the public for making necessary improvements and at the same time guaranteed security to the individual so far as practicable in society. So if public exigencies required the expropriation of the Charles River Bridge, the state had only to comply with the constitution and offer compensation. The proprietors never indicated opposition to such a course of action.

Finally, the proprietors urged rejection of the free bridge proposal on the grounds that it was unwise public policy. They warned that future private investments in internal improvements were at stake. They tied their problem to the current debate on the role of the national government in such projects. Given the growing opposition to federal programs, the proprietors deemed it imperative "that the most liberal encouragement should be held out to *individuals,* in order to induce them to undertake works of public utility, which the government itself has not the means of performing." But they warned that this encouragement essentially rested on the government's ability to keep its faith and adhere to its promises.

By 1827 the battle lines were clear in the legislature. Apparently the free bridge advocates felt confident of the outcome. When a group of legislators—friendly to the free bridge idea, but mindful also of existing property rights—offered proposals for compensation, they were beaten down. The momentum of the free bridge forces temporarily slowed when a committee again rejected their bill, having discerned no necessity for another bridge. This committee, however, seemed to be searching for an acceptable compromise. It recognized the strong community feelings in favor of free avenues to the city, but believed that the bridge owners had valid rights to their tolls. So they suggested that the state buy the stocks of all the bridges and collect tolls until it regained the purchase price with a surplus for a maintenance fund; it could then make the bridges free. The full legislature apparently never considered this proposal. Some free bridge advocates bitterly assailed the idea; the Charles River Bridge proprietors naturally labeled it an "extensive and liberal" plan. In March 1827, however, both the House and Senate ignored compromise proposals and voted to grant a charter to John Skinner and his associates to build a new bridge over the Charles.

The act establishing the Warren Bridge Corporation fixed the termini of the new bridge, setting it apart from the existing one at points of 915 feet on the Boston side of the river, and 260 feet on the Charlestown terminus. The proprietors were to collect tolls until they recovered their investment and expenses. After that, the bridge reverted to the state. In no event were the tolls to be collected after six years. The act also contained the provision noted earlier to the effect that the bridge was not to be built if the Charles River Bridge owners gave notice within sixty days that they would surrender their title to the state by the end of 1831. Immediately following passage of the act, thirty-seven representatives and fourteen senators issued a bitter public protest, charging that the legislation tended to "diminish the confidence in and lessen the security of the rights of private property."

The Charles River Bridge proprietors gained a reprieve on March 10 when Governor Levi Lincoln vetoed the bill. Lincoln had resigned from the state supreme court to run for governor in 1825, but only after assurances that the Federalist and Republican factions alike would support him. After 1825, Lincoln won the governorship for eight yearly terms.

Like his political ally, President John Quincy Adams, Lincoln had a keen interest in governmental promotion of internal improvements, to which he devoted a large part of his first message to the legislature in 1825. He warmly endorsed the development of a canal system by both associations of private individuals and by the government. But in future messages Lincoln consistently urged that attention be directed to the potentialities of the railroads. In 1825 he supported the proposal for a canal between Boston and Albany to link the Bay State with the Erie Canal and the burgeoning western markets; as early as 1827, however, he pressed the legislature to promote a railroad between the two cities. Lincoln regularly voiced concern for Massachusetts' competitive position with surrounding states. In one message he noted that an "immense amount" of local capital was being invested outside the state. He always recognized the state's responsibility for creating a hospitable economic environment. At one point he specifically warned that unless state laws properly encouraged corporations and investments, local improvements would be unnecessarily retarded, if undertaken at all. Largely through his efforts between 1826 and 1830, the legislature altered the liability responsibilities of individual stockholders in corporate enterprises. Gov. wants to encourage investments

Lincoln's veto was the first exercise of that power by a Massachusetts governor. In his message the governor had little to say about the wisdom and need for a new bridge. He did, however, take note of the option which covered the proprietors' surrender of their bridge by the end of 1831. This reinforced his general view of the bill's coercive and misleading intentions. The governor mostly reiterated the earlier arguments against the new bridge. He conceded that public necessity might require the destruction of existing property rights, but was wholly unjustified without compensation. He believed that the proprietors' right to exact tolls was a "vested right upon executed consideration." Therefore the legislature could not destroy "the *right* to toll" without impairing the obligation of the contract. Lincoln also chided the legislators for depriving the owners of the tolls while failing to discharge them from their obligations to maintain the bridge. But the omission of indemnity was at the heart of his veto: "It is alike from these considerations of what is due to *equity* and *public justice,* that the passage of the bill is objected to, as impolitic and inexpedient."

Lincoln's veto message bore down hard on the potential conse-quences of the policy established by the Warren Bridge legislation. Taking note of the increasing antipathy to governmental invest-ments, on both state and national levels, he urged that private corporations be given every encouragement. Above all, he warned that the "good faith of the government," and its "most careful and jealous protection of corporate interests," must be main-tained. If not, private investments would be discouraged, and "the worst policy will be introduced, and the greatest prejudice to country suffered." The House easily overrode the governor's veto on the same day, 99–45. But the more conservative Senate, although voting 16–12 to override, failed of a two-thirds majority and thus sustained the veto.

Lincoln's veto drew warm approbation from prominent figures in Massachusetts. Chief Justice Isaac Parker of the Supreme Judicial Court praised Lincoln for "preserving the public faith from ruthless violation." Daniel A. White told the governor that his veto had saved Massachusetts from disgrace and degradation; the message, he said, was "convincing and satisfactory to all impartial and thinking minds." But for the first time in his guber-natorial career Lincoln encountered organized opposition. Re-publican party caucuses in Suffolk and Middlesex counties as-saulted both the idea of the veto and the inconsistency of the

message. They berated Lincoln's disregard for a legislative determination of the necessity for a new bridge after he himself had
conceded that this was properly a legislative problem. A Boston
group nominated William C. Jarvis, a state representative from
Charlestown, to oppose Lincoln in the forthcoming April elections. Jarvis publicly refused the nomination but nevertheless
drew strong support from Middlesex county. Lincoln easily won
the election with over 75 percent of the vote to Jarvis's 18 percent. The latter, however, carried Middlesex decisively, indicating
the extent of the antagonism and hostility toward the governor
in the area most immediately concerned.

Undaunted by their narrow defeat in the legislative session of
1827, the Warren Bridge promoters resubmitted their bill to the
legislature the following January. The hinterland town of Malden
lent its full support to the Charlestown petitioners, telling the
legislature that the "impediments and hindrances to the travel-
lers" had increased drastically during the last two years. The free
bridge advocates displayed mounting impatience with what they
regarded as the sophistry and obstructive tactics of their opponents. The Boston *American Traveller*, for example, picked up the
Henshaw argument in the South Boston bridge controversy and
insisted that the only vested rights involved were those of the
owners of the banks and flats upon which the new bridge would
have its terminals. The newspaper contemptuously dismissed
Governor Lincoln's concern that the "plighted faith" of the state
was more precious than a thousand bridges. There was only one
issue: whether the public should continue to submit to the inconvenience of a toll bridge. The cause of the free bridge, the
American Traveller confidently concluded, "is the cause of justice,
reason, and the people, and it will prevail." The Charles River
Bridge proprietors wearily remonstrated for the fifth time when
their opponents petitioned the legislature again in January 1828.

The legislative joint committee reversed itself this time, indicating new strength for the Warren Bridge backers. The committee found that "public convenience and necessity" and "public
justice" justified another bridge and recommended a bill to that

effect. Poignant, desperate appeals underlined the proprietors' final protest. They renewed their offer to surrender the franchise with compensation, or to reduce their tolls by one-third. They offered to widen their 42-foot bridge to 60 or 80 feet, to build a circular draw, to widen the access avenues in Charlestown to whatever specifications the legislature desired, and even to build a spur bridge to the westerly part of Boston. The proprietors resorted to the most abject appeasement: "And if there is any other matter or thing (even to the extent of building another bridge) which your memorialists have not specified, in any way pertaining to the convenience and accommodation of the public, they hold themselves ready to accomplish it; thus submitting this whole subject to the discretion of the Legislature, and willingly yielding to them, for all such purposes, the most unqualified power." Finally, they urged the legislature not to sacrifice the property of innocent purchasers—the proverbial "widows and orphans"—who had invested upon the premise of their government's good faith.*

The Warren Bridge bill came before the House on February 5. For the next few weeks friends of the old bridge maneuvered to salvage something. One motion provided that the proprietors would surrender their franchise in eight years. Another proposed to offer $150,000 plus interest for the sale of the bridge. The *American Traveller* assailed both amendments and warned the legislative friends of the new bridge that approval would be tantamount to a concession that the new bridge really was unnecessary. The House decisively defeated both motions, the first by 147–104, and the other by 135–99. One final, but equally fruitless, attempt to do something was an amendment that would have authorized the Charles River Bridge proprietors to construct the new bridge. The bill finally passed the House on February 29, but curiously only by a narrow margin, 133–127. The Senate began consideration of the bill on March 6, and immediately

*According to the proprietors, three-fourths of the bridge shares had changed hands between 1805 and 1828.

rejected, 20-15, a motion to strike the first section calling for a new bridge. Virtually the same lineup held on motions similar to those offered in the House to protect the interest of the Charles River Bridge proprietors. The next day the Senate passed the House bill, but again with a very narrow margin, 19-17. As in the previous session, the proprietors' supporters in both houses entered bitter protests upon the journal after passage. In the Senate ten opponents of the Warren Bridge reiterated their contention that a new bridge was unnecessary, and complained that the legislature had not provided a *"certain remedy"* or *"reasonable compensation"* to the shareholders of the old bridge.

Support for the Warren Bridge was rather evenly distributed on a geographical basis. With the exception of Middlesex, Suffolk, and Worcester counties, the county delegations in the legislature split almost equally on the bill. The Middlesex representatives in the lower house, dominated by the Charlestown group, voted 36-12 in favor of the new bridge. Worcester county's delegates, however, opposed it, 13-25, while Suffolk's representatives, primarily from Boston, also voted against the proposal by a 1-6 margin. Boston was not fully represented during the legislative session. The city was entitled to thirty representatives, but after two elections, dominated by the bridge issue, only six men had gained the necessary majority. The city council then decided against another contest. There were five party lists on the ballot. Although the anti-free bridge forces captured a majority of the total vote, no one ticket consistently had the number of votes necessary to elect its candidates. This stalemate, and Boston's lack of full representation, probably served the free bridge interests.

The new Warren Bridge bill differed little from the previous one. The location and requirements of the bridge were the same; again it was to parallel the existing structure and with virtually similar dimensions. The only stipulation for compensation concerned lands taken for the use and building of the bridge. The state granted the Warren Bridge Corporation the same toll schedule as that of the Charles River Bridge, but with the proviso that after reimbursing the proprietors for building and other expenses, with five per cent interest, the bridge would revert to the commonwealth, in good repair. In any event, the term for taking tolls could not exceed six years. One year after completion, the charter obligated the Warren Bridge proprietors to assume one-half of the annuity paid to Harvard by the Charles River Bridge proprietors. The most significant difference in the 1828 bill was the omission of the stipulation that the bridge would not be built if the Charles River Bridge proprietors surrendered their franchise at an early date. This either implied a new vindictiveness toward the old bridge proprietors or a real conviction that a new bridge was necessary. Either way, the change deprived the proprietors of an important, effective point of contention.

The passage of the 1828 bill was in some ways less decisive than the previous one. It is somewhat surprising therefore that Governor Lincoln signed it. Although he was under tremendous pressure to veto the bill from numerous political allies, along with many prominent Boston lawyers, he bowed to the legislative will. In his 1827 message, Lincoln had conceded the state's right to build a new bridge if public necessity required it. But he had insisted that the "mere relief from tolls" was not sufficient reason, and that the public's need could not be satisfied "by a direct and certain prostration of pre-existing rights, without providing adequate remedies." The 1828 bill certainly provided no remedies for the Charles River Bridge proprietors, the holders of "pre-existing rights"; in fact, the lack of an option for the proprietors to surrender their franchise after a four year grace period in lieu of a new bridge deprived them of even a limited concession from the state. Curiously, this omission may have influenced Lincoln to believe that a new bridge was really necessary. The governor's position, however, was ambiguous at best. In 1827 he had conceded that the determination of necessity was properly a legislative prerogative, but he had pitched his veto to the legislature's failure to provide compensation. In 1828 he let it be known that the legislature was the legitimate judge of necessity, and once it had made its judgment, it was his duty to approve the bill.

Possibly the governor merely submitted to legislative sentiment as expressed in two consecutive years. In addition, executive vetoes were relatively new and suspect. The colonial and revolutionary sentiment against such power undoubtedly still ran quite strong. Indeed, some of the legislators in both houses who had recorded their names on the public protest against the passage of the Warren Bridge bill later voted to override the governor's veto. For these men, institutional loyalties and commitments predominated over policy considerations.

Disappointment, indeed bitterness, with the governor's action characterized the Warren Bridge opponents. Their comments ranged from bewilderment with Lincoln's inconsistency—after all, the bills of 1827 and 1828 were quite similar—to unreserved contempt for his kowtowing to popular sentiments. The *Lowell Journal*, which had supported the claims of the Charles River Bridge proprietors, had predicted a month earlier that he would veto the bill again. After he signed it, the newspaper warned that Lincoln had "prostrated the reputation which has been awarded him by disinterested and intelligent men, and by his obliquity of conduct proved himself undeserving the suffrages of those who regard the character of our State, and the rights which the Constitution gives to our citizens." The *Salem Gazette* charged that Lincoln lacked "firmness and independence" and had simply caved in to popular pressures.

It is difficult to escape the conclusion that Lincoln surrendered his principles to expediency. After his 1827 veto, he told Daniel A. White, a close political ally, that though "the duty was indeed a most painful one," he took great satisfaction that he "had the firmness to meet the occasion, for in the approval of the reflecting and dispassionate... there is a rich reward." But the determination and ferocity of the free bridge movement, coupled with the widespread criticism of his veto and the growing polarization of partisan politics, must have had an effect upon Lincoln by 1828. Institutional limitations aside, Levi Lincoln valued his popularity too much to run counter to political tides.

Although many of the governor's friends remained silent after he signed the bill, the event signalled a great celebration and rejoicing among the citizens of Charlestown and vicinity. The *American Traveller* reported that they "took spirited measures to evince their feelings and manifest their pleasure at the result. Salutes were fired (it is said of 100 guns) at noon and sunset; groups assembled at public places; congratulations were interchanged; the public houses were thrown open and refreshments were served up." The Lowell newspaper, however, labeled the whole celebration as intemperate. The widowed and orphaned Charles River Bridge stockholders offered no public comments.

IV

THE
STATE COURT,
1828-1830

LESS THAN A MONTH after its organization on April 14, 1828, the Warren Bridge Corporation purchased the necessary land sites, and in June began construction of its bridge. Six months later, on Christmas day, the new bridge opened free of toll—for the first day at least. It was over 1700 feet long and was built on seventy-five piers. The carriage path was thirty feet wide, and in addition there were two sidewalks, each seven feet wide. The flooring was of one foot thick hemlock timber and was macadamized with clay and gravel. In virtually all respects it was like its companion, the Charles River Bridge. Its greater popularity, however, was soon apparent. A few weeks after the opening, Massachusetts Senator Edward Everett heard from one of his constituents that the new bridge immediately had three-fourths of the travel. The letter writer could not resist the irony for the conservative Everett: "Fine time for your constituents," he wrote, but "not quite so fine for some of your family friends.... It is really a fine bridge—*though!*" During the first six months of 1829, receipts for the old bridge were down nearly $9,000 from collections of $15,000 for the comparable period of 1828.

As the construction of the bridge began, the Charles River

Bridge proprietors made one last desperate attempt to halt the project. On June 28, Daniel Webster, Lemuel Shaw, and Benjamin Gorham, acting as counsel for the corporation, filed a bill in equity in the Massachusetts Supreme Judicial Court, contending that the Warren Bridge charter impaired the state's earlier obligations and was therefore unconstitutional. Pending a hearing and a final decision on their charges, the attorneys requested an immediate injunction staying the building of the new bridge. The court thereupon granted a hearing for August 5.

The Charles River Bridge lawyers based their plea for an injunction on an 1827 statute providing the court with equity jurisdiction in cases of nuisance. Resorting to the common law of ferries, Webster and Shaw maintained that where a party had exclusive rights, the erection of another ferry nearby constituted a nuisance if it affected the rights of the existing ferry. They did not at this time exactly define the extent of the proprietors' rights except to say that they were entitled to the exclusive right of transportation between Boston and Charlestown. They interpreted the 1785 bridge charter as a substitute for the ancient ferry and as a public contract to operate a specific line of travel. The 1828 Warren Bridge act was therefore unconstitutional because it impaired the obligation of an earlier contract and because it appropriated private property for public use without compensation.

The plaintiffs submitted traditional vested rights propositions that Webster himself had so often and so ably advanced in a series of United States Supreme Court cases. The legislative grant was a contract, and like other contracts, it had to be construed most favorably for the grantee. The plaintiffs applied the common law dictum that a grant carries with it whatever is necessary to enjoy the thing granted. Furthermore, counsel contended that the failure to provide compensation nullified the 1828 legislation. The Bill of Rights of the Massachusetts Constitution and the fifth amendment to the federal constitution, along with a host of judicial precedents, guaranteed that private property could not be taken without consent or compensation.

Webster and Shaw maintained that an injunction was the only

proper and complete remedy if the proprietors' rights had been violated. The injunction would prevent injury before the case could be fully decided on its merits. In addition, it would prevent future suits for damages if the plaintiffs prevailed. They admitted the novelty of injunctions in such cases, but cited a recent New York opinion by Chancellor James Kent fully supporting their position. An injunction, moreover, was the proper remedy as soon as an injury was threatened; this, they contended, was "the peculiar efficacy of a court of chancery, that we thus arrive as near as possible to perfect justice. We are entitled to this interposition until the right in controversy is tried."

Richard Fletcher and William Aylwin replied for the defendants. They argued that the plaintiffs had failed to show a *prima facie* right to exclusive privileges over the river and therefore an injunction was improper. The 1785 charter was merely a license for the proprietors to build the bridge and collect tolls for reimbursement and profit for forty years. The state had not pledged then, or in 1792 when it extended the charter, that it would not make similar grants. They cited the Massachusetts Bill of Rights to show that monopoly claims were not to be favored, and also the common law, which provided that grants by the crown were to be construed beneficially for the crown. Furthermore, the proprietors' claims to exclusive privileges rested on their tenuous succession to the rights of the ferry. But Fletcher and Aylwin noted that the acts of 1785 and 1792 nowhere provided for such a transfer, or for any surceasing of the ferry.

The Warren Bridge counsel maintained that the plaintiffs had a proper remedy by an action in the case. When conflicting rights were at stake, moreover, the courts should not interfere before a trial upon the merits settled the dispute. They also argued that Webster and Shaw had misconstrued the 1827 statute providing equity jurisdiction for the court in nuisance cases. That law, they said, used nuisance in the popular sense, meaning such as those that affected life or health, and that the legislature certainly did not intend it to cover cases of conflicting rights. They reminded the justices of the unpopularity of chancery jurisdiction and equity courts throughout Massachusetts' history and that it would be unwise for the court to extend its jurisdiction on its own initiative.

A few days after the hearing the court unanimously rejected the plaintiffs' motion for an injunction. But Chief Justice Isaac Parker, speaking for the court, emphasized that this decision was not made on the merits of the controversy. He expressed regret that the court could not immediately pass upon all the questions and resolve the issue. But whatever was lost by delay, he believed was compensated by "the security and stability" resulting from cautious and formal deliberation.

Parker's opinion from the outset revealed a reluctance to assume judicial power by implication. During the oral arguments he, too, observed that chancery courts always had been an object of suspicion in Massachusetts. Moreover, he must have been mindful that popular dissatisfaction with appointive lifetime judiciaries was a recurring phenomenon. Parker's reticence undoubtedly reflected the current Massachusetts political turmoil, with its upsurge of Jacksonian sentiment.

The Charles River Bridge proprietors had based their pleas for an injunction upon the recent 1827 statute that provided that the Supreme Judicial Court could "hear and determine in equity any matter touching waste or nuisance in which there is not a plain, adequate and complete remedy at law." Defining the legislature's meaning of "nuisance," Parker disagreed with the defendants' counsel that this only concerned public matters affecting the life, health, or comfort of the community. He believed that the jurisdiction also covered nuisances strictly private, such as an unlawful interference with a preexisting right, the interruption of light or air, the diverting of water, or the subduction of profits from a mill or ferry. Where the right to enjoyment of such things was "clear and uncontroverted," said Parker, and effectual relief or compensation doubtful, the mischief could be stopped by an injunction. As was done throughout the years of litigation in the Charles River Bridge Case, Parker analogized the common law of ferries to bridges. Thus he contended that establishing a ferry without right so near to an existing one with vested rights as to diminish the latter's profits was a nuisance.

Turning next to the meaning of a "plain, adequate, and complete" remedy, Parker applied the phrase to the alleged facts in the case. The old bridge proprietors enjoyed a franchise from the state, designed for service and profit, and for which they gave a valuable consideration. The defendants, allegedly without authority, erected a bridge so near as to diminish certainly the profits of the other. Although the other party could institute a common law action for injury and a recovery of damages, the injury would remain and the damages would be uncertain. "Nothing short of an absolute prevention of the evil is a complete remedy," Parker observed, "and a court of common law is incompetent to afford this." The court thus found the plaintiffs' plea as within the meaning of the 1827 legislation, and that it therefore had jurisdiction in the case. But having established jurisdiction, Parker warily approached granting the injunction itself. He recognized, for example, that it seemed to be a "novel application" to impose an injunction upon a party who had not been able to fully answer the charges.

The chief precedents for such an injunction came from English and New York chancery courts. But they were relatively new. In a 1752 English case, the judge had indignantly dismissed a motion for an injunction, calling it unprecedented and extraordinary. Furthermore, most of the earlier cases were almost free of controversy or dispute. Parker deduced two constant principles for judicial guidance from the precedents: first, that urgent necessity be required; and second, that the complainants' rights be clear and incontrovertible.* In the opinion of the court, the

---

*The most commonly cited injunction precedent by the plaintiffs was Kent's opinion in *Jerome and others* v. *Ross* (7 Johnson's Chancery Reports 315, 1823). In his last decision as Chancellor, Kent dissolved a lower court injunction in a trespass action. While his actual decision was adverse to the Charles River Bridge proprietors' cause, Webster and Shaw projected Kent's criteria for justifying injunctions as applicable to their case. Kent had said that injunctions could be issued when there was irreparable injury to the property such that it no longer could be used for its original purpose, when there was destruction of the inheritance value of the property, when there was destruction of one's trade or livelihood, or when there was permanency of the trespass. Perhaps Kent's most famous use of an injunction was in the great steamboat monopoly case, *Ogden* v. *Gibbons* (1820).

Charles River Bridge proprietors failed to establish a *prima facie* case on either point.

Parker noted the proprietors' claim that they had a lawful charter giving them the exclusive privilege to build and maintain the bridge between Boston and Charlestown. If true, then they were entitled to an immediate injunction. But the exclusive right claim was the turning point in the whole controversy, and the defendants hotly disputed the proprietors' contention. It was not, therefore, "clear and incontrovertible" that the defendants had proceeded under an act that unconstitutionally impaired the obligation of an earlier contract. Similarly, Parker said that the plaintiffs' plea for compensation depended upon the nature of the 1785 charter. "[I]t does not become us," the Chief Justice concluded, "on a question discretionary in its nature to decide so promptly against a deliberate act of the legislature."

Parker closed his opinion on a note of warning to all who were interested in the result and might seek speculative profits. The validity of the Warren Bridge grant remained an open and undecided question. The denial of the injunction, he cautioned, should not encourage the schemes of those who either sought to maintain or overthrow the old bridge. The issues were complex, and the competing claims could only be resolved by a full and lengthy airing of all available facts.

Eighty years afterward, the historian Charles Warren found it surprising that the court denied a preliminary injunction before the filing of an answer, on the grounds that it was "novel" and "startling." In Warren's time preliminary injunctions were commonplace, especially against the activities of organized labor. By then courts granted restraining injunctions with impunity, and often on the basis of *ex parte* hearings. That Parker and his colleagues acted so cautiously testifies to the contemporary novelty of the doctrine and perhaps also to their recognition of the judiciary's precarious standing, particularly in its equity role.

During the half century after 1800 critics periodically questioned the quality of the bench and the role of judicial power in the democratic process. Jeffersonian and Jacksonian rhetoric par-

no injuction because of status of the courts

ticularly focused attention on the political attitudes and roles of judges. The judicial independence guaranteed in the federal and state constitutions was hardly absolute or secure. Political realists always recognized the political and policy roles of the courts. Jefferson, for example, observed in 1801 that the Federalists, defeated at the polls, had retreated into the judiciary to batter down the works of Republicanism. Those in political ascendancy, however, did not ignore or take lightly the political potential of the courts. During the early 1800s, on both the national and state levels, there were several attempts to remove judges by impeachment proceedings. In nearly every case political opposition motivated the action. While most failed, they proved instructive. In exchange for their independence judges retreated somewhat from extreme political activities, especially when they ran counter to popular trends. Still, in the decades prior to the Civil War, the trend toward an elected judiciary gained momentum.

Within such a framework it undoubtedly would have been foolhardy for the Massachusetts Supreme Judicial Court to throw a novel and drastic roadblock in the path of a powerful local political movement. Free bridge proponents were not the kind of people who looked with favor upon an aristocratic anachronism such as an appointed, lifetime judiciary. There also was a chance of alienating a legislature that had only recently increased the court's equity jurisdiction. To use it so soon afterward to thwart the legislature's wishes in a matter where the legal issues were clouded would indeed have been chancy business. The judges were satisfied, and correctly so, that the plaintiffs still had an adequate remedy in an action of law against the Warren Bridge. An injunction provided only a limited legal gain for the proprietors; but the political risks for the court were simply immense.

Following the injunction proceedings, the Warren Bridge proprietors filed their formal answer to the plaintiffs' bill in November 1828. The next month produced supplemental bills by both sides and the respective lawyers began to take depositions in the case. The plaintiffs repeatedly pressed for an early hearing of their case. But the defense just as regularly sought delay, probably to give their bridge time to win public favor. Finally, in October 1829, almost one year after the opening of the new bridge, the court heard arguments on the merits of the case.

Both sides maintained their earlier positions, but now elaborated them a great deal. The opposing counsel clashed sharply on the meaning of the 1785 charter and particularly on the question of whether or not it granted exclusive privileges to the plaintiffs. In dismissing the plea for an injunction, Chief Justice Parker had observed that this was the crucial point in the whole issue. The lawyers accordingly took their cue. They advanced extensive interpretations of the charter and linked their construction to the general questions of public policy and internal improvements.

For the plaintiffs, Shaw reiterated his earlier contention that the 1785 charter gave the Charles River Bridge proprietors successor rights to the ferry's exclusive privileges. Beyond that, he insisted the legislature intended that the grant be a beneficial one. The bridge was a work of public utility, but one of great risk to the investors. They were to build and maintain it, pay an annuity to the college, and then surrender the bridge to the government in good repair after a number of years. The toll, he said, was for their "sole benefit" to reimburse them for their expenses. Shaw argued that these tolls were the substance of the grant and the proprietors' only real security. If the grant was a beneficial one, then the tolls must be safeguarded absolutely and made exclusive. Although the act establishing the new bridge did not take away the plaintiffs' franchise, it destroyed the essence, the only tangible property, of the franchise. In this manner, Shaw argued that the state's action was repugnant to the federal constitution because it impaired the obligation of an existing contract, and repugnant to the Massachusetts constitution because it expropriated private property for public use without compensation.

In support, Webster called upon the court to boldly correct legislative excesses and affirm traditional doctrines regarding public contracts. He particularly pointed to the common law notion that the legislature could not indirectly do what it could not do directly. The fact that the legislature had, in effect, destroyed the plaintiffs' franchise, Webster said, was more important than any legal subtleties that denied the claims of exclusive privilege. Finally, Webster assailed the idea that "public necessity" and "public convenience" offered adequate justification for the legislature's action. He betrayed his suspicion and disdain for popular feeling and fickle majorities when he contrasted them with what he regarded as the eternal truths of the law. "Public necessity is apt to be public feeling," he warned, "and on this rock we are in danger of making shipwreck of the bill of rights." He denied the necessity for a new bridge and insisted that, even if the need existed, it was an irrelevant point upon which to try the case. Unfortunately for Webster, notions of "necessity" and "convenience" were not irrelevant to either legislatures or courts and, for both, such ideas proved decisive.

The defense, in reply, similarly expanded upon its earlier contentions. The 1785 charter established that the proprietors could form a corporation for forty years and take tolls for their sole benefit. This, the defense counsel argued, was the whole of the proprietors' exclusive rights. They agreed that the legislature could not resume what it had granted earlier. But they vigorously denied that the legislature had granted the Charles River Bridge proprietors exclusive rights of travel between Boston or Charlestown, or that it had abdicated its right to charter other bridges. Furthermore, counsel suggested that the proprietors themselves had denied their exclusive privileges and acknowledged the state's rights when they accepted an extension of their own charter after the state had authorized the West Boston Bridge in 1792.

The opposing counsel sought to relate their legal arguments to larger considerations of public policy. Shaw and Webster solemnly warned that public enterprise would come to a halt if private capital could not trust the government to keep its faith and honor its contracts. Fletcher, on the other hand, attached the stigma of monopoly to the proprietors' claims and insisted that the "genius of monopoly" always imposed a restraint on enterprise. The "free course of legislation" and liberal competition were at stake, he argued. Progress dictated that new forms or inventions would always injure old ones, but that, Fletcher said, was a necessary price for promoting the general welfare. In a sarcastic parting shot, Webster hotly defended the necessity for monopoly. "Doubtless our predecessors, the Indians, had the perfect freedom of competition which the defendants now want to introduce; but they had no bridges, no ferries." Webster maintained that "all the public improvements in the country" had been carried out by monopoly, "from a grant by the public, of security for private funds, for the benefit of using them." Obdurately, almost arrogantly, Webster ignored the popular, the legislative, and the defense counsel's contention that vested rights, in the judgment of the community, can outlive their usefulness and must succumb to newer and larger demands of public policy.

There were many issues at stake in the Charles River Bridge case, but once the controversy shifted from the legislative battleground to the judicial arena, a constant, pervasive, and quite subtle question of institutional power became apparent. Simply phrased, the question was whether legislatures or courts would determine the important ingredients of fact and need involved in the formulation of public policy. In his presentation, Webster anticipated later nineteenth and twentieth century developments by expressly inviting the judiciary to substitute its judgment when the legislature, as a result of political pressures, acted irresponsibly and unwisely. He contended that a significant number of legislators had voted for the Warren Bridge bill purely out of political expediency, but had been dubious as to its constitutionality. These men, Webster argued, confidently expected the judiciary to resolve the constitutional questions. Webster seemed sympathetic to the predicament of legislators who voted for legislation of doubtful constitutionality; the nature of their function involved greater concern for the needs of the larger community as opposed to the rights of the individual. But judicial tribunals, he maintained, were best suited "for the investigation of difficult questions of private rights," and should therefore resolve their constitutional doubts in favor of the individual citizens involved.

He boldly appealed to the pride and dignity of the American judge and what he called the judiciary's special privilege of being the final arbiter of constitutional questions.

Webster's proposition confronted the judiciary with a nagging problem of judicial role, and the attendant considerations of the limits to judicial power. After the legislature chartered the new bridge, judicial relief was the only recourse left to the Charles River Bridge proprietors. The numerous judges who eventually heard the case both in the state court and in the United States Supreme Court, acknowledged Webster's challenge. Their individual conception of judicial role in turn largely dictated their response to the substantive issues.

In January 1830 the Massachusetts court announced a decree in favor of the defendants, although the four judges divided evenly on the validity of the 1828 legislation. But the complaint was dismissed so that an appeal could be taken to the United States Supreme Court.† The judges delivered their opinions *seriatim.* Justices Marcus Morton and Samuel Wilde rejected the claims of the old bridge proprietors, while Chief Justice Isaac Parker and Associate Justice Samuel Putnam, in differing ways, held that the state had impaired the obligation of its contract with the proprietors.

Morton's opinion was particularly important. He concentrated on the broad question of charter construction and public policy, and thus established a new aspect to the case. It was also the one that ultimately dominated the future clashes in the United States Supreme Court. Charles Warren labelled Morton "a robust Democrat of the radical type." Whatever that may mean, Morton was certainly the state's most prominent Jacksonian Democrat. He was a congressman from 1817 to 1821; he was elected Lieutenant Governor in 1824, and was raised to the Supreme Court the next year. He served on the court for fifteen years, and during that time was a perennial gubernatorial candidate. He was finally

† Section 25 of the Judiciary Act of 1789 provided that the Supreme Court could take appeals only if state courts sustained state laws challenged as repugnant to the federal constitution.

elected in 1839 and again in 1843. In the 1850s he led a number of his Democratic followers into the new Free Soil party.

Morton's opinion reflected and employed the emerging ideas of liberal competition. His language unmistakably matched much of the Jacksonian rhetoric of the day. He was vitally concerned with progress and resented any vested rights that would interfere with the community's quest for material improvements. Morton fully accepted the defendants' arguments. The charter, he said, had not granted exclusive rights to the proprietors and the legislature retained the power to authorize other bridges over the Charles River. The new bridge admittedly diverted some of the tolls from the old, but the damages were merely consequential and neither the defendants nor the state were liable for them.

Morton feared that the channels of communication, business, and the condition of the community in general would stagnate and atrophy if the courts recognized all implied claims of exclusive rights or privileges. Further internal improvements might be impeded; improved roads, new bridges, canals, and railroads might be legally blocked because all improvements potentially diminished the profits of older corporations or forms of property. Morton therefore insisted that public contracts be strictly construed in order then to insure progress for the community and the protection of its interest. He conceded that corporate rights and privileges expressly granted should be enforced, but maintained that a broad construction of charters, and particularly a reading of implied rights and privileges into them, threatened the community's future welfare. If possible, courts should always adopt a limited and restricted construction of charters, rather than impute "such improvidence" to the legislature.

The Charles River Bridge charter, of course, had no expressed grant of exclusive privileges, thus giving Morton his opportunity to reject the plaintiffs' pleas for a liberal construction. Their interpretation, he said, amounted "substantially to a covenant, that during the plaintiffs' charter an important part of our Commonwealth, as to facilities for travel and transportation, should remain *in statu quo*." Morton found such construction inconsistent with sound reason, judicial precedents, the nature of legislation, and "the principles of our free institutions." He admitted the necessity and usefulness of exclusive rights for a short period; but they usually tended, he observed, to impede further improvements and interrupt equal competition. He thus recognized strict construction as the means for keeping claims of privilege within tight bounds and for complementing the traditional policy of encouraging internal improvements by fair competition.

Morton curtly dismissed the Shaw-Webster argument that future enterprises would come to a halt if investors could not feel secure in the enjoyment of their property. He maintained that businessmen could confidently rely on the legislature not to sacrifice the property of one portion of the community for the benefit of another. The constitution still protected private property from legislative expropriation without compensation. If these were not sufficient safeguards, justifying capital risks, then the Charles River Bridge proprietors were at fault for not having negotiated a more favorable bargain and for not having obtained more explicit rights from the state.

The legislative and judicial history of the Charles River Bridge controversy is often cast into a neat dichotomy between the new Jacksonian Democrats of the "radical type," as Charles Warren characterized them, and old-line Federalists, or new Whigs in Federalist clothing. But Justice Samuel Wilde, a Federalist, endorsed Morton's opinion throughout, and added some ideas of his own. Probably Wilde's opinion was the least doctrinaire of the four. First, he noted that there were no exclusive privileges in the charter; furthermore, he maintained that when the Charles River Bridge proprietors accepted an extension of their charter at the time of the West Boston Bridge, they negated all claims to exclusiveness. Wilde primarily focused on the original intent of the Charles River Bridge charter, which he then linked to the legislature's 1828 action. The declared object of the 1785 grant, he said, was "the public accommodation," and from this he implied that the community was 'at all events to be accommodated." Wilde believed that the new bridge authorization in 1828 was a legislative determination that the public convenience and necessity required an additional avenue. Significantly, this "old Federalist" completely bowed to legislative prerogative. The courts, he said, could not determine necessity. And whether the proprietors' counteroffers were reasonable or not (and Wilde thought they were) was also beyond judicial competence.

Justice Putnam, another old line Federalist, had been Joseph Story's law tutor and a member of the court since 1814. His opinion was an impassioned plea for the maintenance of vested rights and sustained the Webster-Shaw arguments on every point. He directly confronted and refuted Morton's arguments for a strict construction of charters. "In the construction of contracts," Putnam wrote, "the law regards the subject matter more than the manner; the substance more than the form; the spirit more than the letter." The conclusion was inescapable: tolls were the substance of the proprietors' property and the legislature could not lawfully destroy them. The spirit of the contract granted exclusive privileges, chiefly the right to collect tolls for passage between Boston and Charlestown. The legislature, he believed, had done indirectly what it could not do directly. Putnam dismissed the state's rights in the matter as mere sophistry: "It would be in vain to tell the proprietors that their franchise remained, notwithstanding a new bridge had been placed in effect side by side, which should deprive the old bridge of its emoluments."

Chief Justice Parker's opinion was perhaps the most interesting. In 1827, it will be recalled, Parker had warmly praised Governor Lincoln's veto of the Warren Bridge bill. Now he found himself caught on the horns of a dilemma between his view of legal requirements on the one hand, and his understanding of sound public policy. Much of his discussion followed Morton's conclusions on the rights of the Charles River Bridge proprietors and the state. But he nevertheless found reason for compensation and consequently held the act creating a new bridge unconstitutional.

Parker agreed that the college s rights had not been transferred to the bridge proprietors and that their grant was not an exclusive one. He admitted that when public exigencies demanded, the government had a right to establish a new bridge. He also acknowledged that changes and improvements often damaged existing property interests; still, there had never been provision for compensation. Losses of this kind, he said, were the general effect of such legislation, property being "in fact held upon a tenure which admits of its deterioration in value from causes of this kind." Like Morton, Parker recognized the inevitability of progress and its consequent damage to some types of property; he similarly acknowledged the ultimate effect as usually beneficial to the whole community.

But Parker insisted that the forms of property had to be distinguishable if one were to destroy the other. Canals and railroads could understandably be established against turnpikes, and bridges could succeed to ferry rights. In both cases a qualitative difference in the property form existed, implying a technological improvement and benefit for the whole community. But when the legislature chartered any similar franchise within a few rods of an existing one, such as had been done with the Warren Bridge, then the first operators were entitled to an indemnity; otherwise, they might maintain an action for damages. Interestingly enough, Parker admitted he could not support his doctrine with precedents or authorities. But it was, he believed, a "reasonable" one, grounded "on the principles of our government and constitution, and on the immutable principles of justice, which ought to bind governments as well as people." In effect, Parker tried to cut a neat line between two divergent views of public policy. He conceded the governmental right to determine public needs and at the same time provide for individual security. Such a policy, he argued, offered justice both to the public and the investor. Finally, he rejected any suggestion that the costs to the community would be too high and that public improvements would be impeded. Progress and growth would suffer, Parker concluded, if investors had constantly to fear the loss or impairment of their property.

Thus on the basis of his own rationalization of a requirement for compensation, Parker found that the act authorizing the Warren Bridge was unconstitutional. But at bottom, the Chief

Justice recognized the political, rather than the constitutional, character of the problem. He observed that the whole question of indemnification was prejudiced because of the old bridge s great profits. If the legislature had chartered a new bridge in 1787, a year after the opening of the Charles River Bridge, without indemnification for the latter, Parker believed it would have been universally condemned as unjust. He was correct.

#   #   #

The division within the state court encouraged the Charles River Bridge proprietors to appeal to the United States Supreme Court. They filed an application for a writ of error two days after the state court's decision. It was granted on March 19, with arguments set for the following January term. As the case moved into the national arena, the issues and interests affecting the immediate plaintiffs and defendants developed larger meaning. On one level, the Charles River Bridge controversy involved the vested rights of the old bridge proprietors and the interests working for a free bridge. But after 1830, the question of bridges was only a cover for the problems and higher stakes involving railroad development.

In October 1826, George Stephenson successfully demonstrated his steam locomotive in England. Reports of the event soon reached the United States and a rush followed for legislative charters to build railroads. Baltimore businessmen, for example, anxious to capture western markets, obtained a state charter for the Baltimore and Ohio Railroad in 1828. But the construction and use of canals was just reaching its zenith at the time, and canal owners naturally resisted encroachments by the new competition. Railroad speculators, supported by mercantile interests who complained of canal monopolies and high rates, advocated public sanction for railroads. Counterattacking the arguments of vested and preexisting rights advanced by the canal interests, they pressed for public charters on the grounds of desirable public policy. Significantly, they assaulted the constitutional claims of the canals with ideas similar to those articulated by Justice Morton in the Charles River Bridge case.

In one sense, the legislative action and judicial precedent in the bridge controversy cleared the way for the railroads. Legally and constitutionally the barriers impeding technological progress were down. Yet there is evidence that in Massachusetts, at least, the bridge action frightened private investors and therefore they were reluctant to purchase railroad stocks. Soon after the state court's decision, the legislature considered a petition to charter a railroad between Boston and Lowell, paralleling the Middlesex Canal. The legislative bill proposed that the state would not charter another railroad for the same route, but the House of Representatives, in an antimonopoly mood, struck the provision. The petitioners then withdrew their bill, according to the *Boston Daily Advertizer* because they "were not inclined to take a charter on terms which would subject them to all the expense of making the experiment of building the first railroad without any chance of profit from it." Without this guarantee, the newspaper added, nobody was "disposed to subscribe to the stock." The *Essex Gazette* warned that after the bridge affair, no private financiers would support railroads or any other public enterprises without a monopoly guarantee for a specific period of time. A few years later, in 1835, Josiah Quincy, Jr. complained how difficult it was to sell stock subscriptions for the western railroads because many investors had "no faith in legislative grants of charters since the fate of the Charlestown bridge."

At first glance, then, the direful warnings of the Charles River Bridge proprietors concerning the future of public enterprises appeared prophetic. But their misfortune was instructive and a blessing in disguise for potential railroad investors. In January 1830, the legislature, dominated by areas that stood to gain little from anticipated railroad construction, rejected the idea of state financial participation. Boston merchants, along with western farmers and manufacturers, who stood to gain most from railroads, were simply overwhelmed in the legislature. Significantly, Middlesex County farmers who probably favored the free bridge access to Boston for marketing purposes opposed a public policy that would improve the marketing ability of their western competitors. The coastal areas outside Boston saw little potential in the railroads for themselves and naturally opposed being taxed for such enterprise. If railroads were to be developed, the impetus would have to come from unsubsidized private sources. But the bridge controversy brought about an understandable caution and reluctance on the part of private investors.

Matters were thus at an impasse. The state simply could not tolerate a situation that threatened to retard economic progress or impair its competitive position with surrounding areas. Widespread despair and concern prevailed regarding the state's all too apparent stagnation. Population growth relative to some other eastern states, and the new western ones, lagged. In 1830 Massachusetts ranked eighth in population, down from its second position of 1790. Furthermore, Boston was not only envious of, but was actually threatened by, the success of the Erie Canal, by means of which New York City had come to dominate western markets. As long as the state itself refused to supply investment capital, private investors held the whip hand. Confronted then by both pressures from potential investors and the obvious needs of the state, the legislature capitulated on the issue of charter guarantees. Indeed, the state granted charters on terms perhaps better than anyone might have expected before 1828 or, at least, during the height of the bridge controversy. The legislature dramatized the sudden turnabout of affairs in 1831 when it issued a charter for the Boston and Worcester Railroad—with a thirty year guarantee of exclusive privileges on the line of travel. Public subscriptions of railroad stocks at first were disappointing, but innate caution toward a new enterprise, and the promise of more lucrative returns from manufacturing enterprises, offer more of an explanation than any imagined fears of legislative expropriation. Significantly, Boston and New York bankers cheerfully assumed the risks.

Justice Morton had remarked that the Charles River Bridge proprietors had been remiss for not having negotiated a more certain and favorable contract with the state. Their fate undoubtedly was an instructive lesson for other investors. But there was also a lesson regarding the limits of public power when the community was dependent upon private initiative and resources for development. Thus the balance of power was struck in an ironic way: witness the spectacle of the strict construction doctrine that sought to suppress monopoly claims in behalf of community well-being and progress, but only incited the development of other monopolies, again in the name of the community and progress. The community alternately dispensed its favors and vented its wrath on corporate enterprise like a capricious courtesan.

(a) railroads, state can't afford to undertake

(b) so give exclusive charters to private investors who are scared because of Bridge controversy

V

THE
SUPREME COURT,
1831-1835

THE UNITED STATES SUPREME COURT first heard arguments on the Charles River Bridge case in early March 1831.
To be sure, that body was a familiar one to Daniel Webster and
the other lawyers in the case; for Webster, moreover, it was a
reliable one. Although Andrew Jackson had appointed two new
justices during his two years as president, a majority of the Court
dated from James Madison's first presidential term. For over
twenty years, most of these men had sat together in judgment of
the great constitutional controversies decided by the Court.
This was still a John Marshall court, albeit somewhat weakened
in doctrinal and personal cohesion. The venerable Chief Justice
had served for three decades and he remained the Court's dominant figure. Marshall's intellectual powers seemed undiminished,
and his views on the nature of the federal union and the supremacy
of the Constitution were as firm as when John Adams placed him
on the Court in 1801. He was the major living representative of
those Federalist principles that had guided and sustained the Constitution of 1787. Much of the earlier political antagonism toward
Marshall had disappeared in this twilight of his career. He was
venerated by the public as a hero and patriot from the Revolution

and the early days of the republic. He was esteemed by the legal community for his judicial efforts. By 1831 Marshall enjoyed a popularity that would have been unimaginable during the days of his great political duels with his kinsman, Thomas Jefferson.

Next to Marshall in point of service was his sometime antagonist, William Johnson of South Carolina. As Jefferson's first appointee to the high court, Johnson had been expected to resist the centralizing and vested rights ideas then prevalent among the Federalist judges. But while Johnson established his historical reputation as the first great dissenter on the Court, his differences with Marshall and his colleagues were usually ones of degree and not of kind. At times he went beyond the Chief Justice: in *Gibbons* v. *Ogden*, for example, and in the Delaware Dam case, he favored plenary federal control over interstate commerce; and in *Fletcher* v. *Peck*, he stressed natural law principles for the protection of property rights. It is ironic also that Johnson was in the vanguard of Unionist opposition to nullification in his native state. In failing health, partly because of the strains of the nullification fight, Johnson attended court sessions in Washington only sporadically before his death in 1834.

Marshall's closest intellectual and personal companion was Joseph Story of Massachusetts, one of the most learned lawyers and constitutional commentators ever to sit on the court. Although appointed by Madison in 1811 as a "Jeffersonian Republican," Story never wavered in his devotion to national supremacy and the primacy of property rights. Almost filial-pietistic toward Marshall, Story shared the Chief Justice's concerns and principles and the two men functioned in virtually perfect tandem. After Marshall's death in 1835, and the rapid transformation of the Court's personnel, Story found himself almost alone or, as he described it, the last of the "old race of judges." In that position he regularly voted against the new directions of judicial behavior, constantly invoking the words or opinions of Marshall in support of his own.

Gabriel Duvall of Maryland and Smith Thompson of New York filled out the older group. Madison had appointed Duvall in 1811 also; like Story, he neatly complemented Marshall's views.

Thompson was a veteran of the New York Supreme Court; appointed by Monroe in 1823, he was the newcomer to the group. Throughout his judicial career, Thompson revealed a strong concern for property rights and for the powers of the state governments, particularly when they conflicted with federal regulation of interstate commerce.

John McLean of Ohio and Henry Baldwin of Pennsylvania were the new Jackson appointees. The President named McLean in 1829 primarily because he was anxious to relieve McLean as Postmaster General. McLean had served in the same post under John Quincy Adams and had refused to implement Jackson's instructions to remove Adams' supporters from his department. He had presidential ambitions as well, and Jackson hoped the Supreme Court post would end his maneuverings. Unfortunately, it did not, and for the next three decades McLean actively sought the presidential nomination, first from the Whigs, and then from the Republicans. He was a singular character. He was never wholly in sympathy with Marshall and Story, and later on was even less so with Marshall's successor, Roger B. Taney. Baldwin succeeded Bushrod Washington in 1831, and his nomination pleased even John Quincy Adams, who rarely found any Jackson act acceptable, let alone wise. Brilliant but erratic, Baldwin, like McLean, was essentially a loner on the bench.

The Supreme Court of 1831, then, was a veteran body. The justices averaged sixty-one years in age, and better than fifteen years service; four of the seven had had a tenure of more than twenty years. Geographically, the older states still dominated the Court; only McLean of Ohio came from one of the states formed after the adoption of the Constitution. Most important, however, a majority of the Court had sat together, and had acted in concert, on most of the great constitutional issues of the preceding decades. In this respect, counsel in the Charles River Bridge Case could not help but notice that these justices had invariably interpreted the contract clause of the Constitution in such a way as to restrain state interference with property rights.

The justices, excepting the absent Duvall, heard arguments during the week of March 7. Webster and Warren Dutton appeared for the plaintiffs while Attorney General William Wirt and Walter Jones represented the Warren Bridge proprietors. While the *Washington National Intelligencer* described the case as one of "much importance," and noted that "giants are in the field," the more dramatic issues being argued concurrently in the Cherokee Nation and Georgia case overshadowed it in public attention. The bridge arguments concluded on March 11; five days later, the Court announced that it was unable to agree on a judgment and ordered the case continued. John Marshall and his colleagues never reached a final decision, however, and the case lingered in a kind of limbo until a largely reconstituted court heard new arguments six years later.

The reasons for the deadlock and indecision within the Marshall Court are uncertain. Justices Story and Thompson definitely favored the Charles River Bridge proprietors after the first arguments, as they did six years later. In late 1831 Story prepared a draft opinion supporting the plaintiffs' claims. But in March 1832 he reluctantly admitted failure to gain a majority, saying that the Court was "greatly divided in opinion and it is not certain what the finale will be." Justice Baldwin later asserted that he alone favored the claims of the Warren Bridge and the state. It is safe to assume that Justice McLean insisted in 1831, as he did in 1837, that the Court had no jurisdiction. Duvall was absent during the arguments, having been called away by his wife's illness. The precise opinions of Marshall and Johnson are shrouded in vagueness. If both had subscribed to Story's opinion, then the plaintiffs would have had a narrow majority in their favor. But one—or both—obviously stood with McLean in denying jurisdiction, or possibly with Baldwin in favor of the defendants.

The common assumption is that Marshall, as usual, agreed with Story, but there is no direct evidence. Story himself never explicitly claimed Marshall as an unqualified ally in the case. And given the Chief Justice's opinion in an 1830 contract clause case, and certain clues in the Court's calendar and minutes, it is quite probable that Marshall had some doubts as to the claims of the Charles River Bridge people.*

Obviously troubled by the case, the Court accepted a motion for reargument in early 1833. But it did nothing and the case continued on the docket as the last "Marshall Court" rapidly disintegrated. Johnson died in August 1834; Duvall submitted his resignation a few months later; Marshall died in Philadelphia in July 1835. Thus, in less than a year, Andrew Jackson found himself with three vacancies to fill on the Court. Naturally, he determined to make it more "democratick."

Marshall's admirers were inconsolable. His death and the other vacancies on the Court caused consternation and despair among Whigs and conservatives generally. With self-righteous fervor the *National Intelligencer* recognized Jackson's opportunity and complained that the chief justiceship would be another "one of the spoils which the ravenous clutches of party may seize and appropriate to its sordid purposes." Marshall's erstwhile critics mostly allowed the occasion to pass with polite words and praise for an older type of patriot. Hezekiah Niles, a southern editor who in the past had been bitingly critical of Marshall's nationalistic opinions, now admitted that only Washington commanded more "reverence and homage of the heart [from] . . . the American people." But William Leggett of the *New York Evening Post,* a spokesman for the radical Democrats, wasted little sentiment and frankly welcomed Marshall's passing as an opportunity for "the cause of democratick principles." While regretting the demise of an "eminent and exemplary man," he was "pleased that he [was] . . . removed at last"; Leggett, moreover, felt no cause to "grieve that the cause of aristocracy [had] lost one of its chief supports."

Jackson proceeded to fill the first vacancies in January 1835, a few months after Johnson's death. The only limitation upon Jackson's latitude was the tradition that the nominee be a resident of the circuit he would have to serve. Jackson's earlier appointments of

*See Note, pp. 173-180 for further comment.

McLean and Baldwin had been dictated in part by political obligations or expediency; but now, nearing the end of his presidency, Jackson operated under few restraints. On January 5 he nominated James M. Wayne of Georgia to succeed Johnson. Significantly, Jackson by-passed a number of prominent South Carolinians in selecting Wayne, a former Democratic congressman and a staunch foe of nullification. Wayne's congressional connections, and particularly his Unionist sympathies, made him acceptable to divergent factions, including the usually vigilant Whigs. The contemporary faith in Wayne's nationalist sentiments were later justified, for he loyally remained on the Court during the Civil War, though he suffered personal losses and ostracism in his native Georgia.

Ten days later, and before Marshall's death, Jackson boldly nominated Roger Brooke Taney of Maryland to succeed Duvall. If the Whigs found Wayne tolerable, the choice of Taney could not have been more calculated to arouse their animus and wrath. Despite his Federalist origins, and his relatively moderate views among the Jacksonian advisors, Taney epitomized to the Whigs the Administration's radicalism and high-handed arrogance. The opposition never forgave him for his role—his servility, as they characterized it—in the Bank War. After two successive Secretaries of the Treasury had refused to follow Jackson's order to remove federal deposits from the Bank of the United States, Taney moved into the post and loyally executed Administration policy. The Whigs took some measure of satisfaction when the Senate refused to confirm Taney's Treasury appointment. In March, 1835 the Whigs retaliated further and blocked Taney's appointment to the Court. It is ironic, however, that Chief Justice Marshall endorsed the allegedly radical and irresponsible Taney, and volunteered favorable information in Taney's behalf to a Virginia senator.

Marshall died four months after Taney's rejection. Democratic politicians and spokesmen, clamoring for revenge, overwhelmingly called for Taney's nomination. The Whigs accordingly feared for the worst. Finally, on December 28, 1835, Jackson submitted Taney's name to the Senate for Marshall's place, along with Philip

B. Barbour of Virginia to succeed Duvall. Even Charles Warren, hardly an admirer of either Taney or Jacksonian Democracy, in his history of the Court remarked that the Whigs reacted to Taney's appointment "with very bad grace." The *New York American,* for example, complained that "the pure ermine of the Supreme Court is sullied by the appointment of that political hack, Roger B. Taney." More pathetic was Webster's report that Justice Story thought "the Supreme Court is *gone* and I think so too." And Barbour certainly did not give Administration opponents any comfort either. John Quincy Adams earlier had described the Virginian as a "shallow-pated wild-cat . . . fit for nothing but to tear the Union to rags and tatters."

The Senate confirmed Taney's appointment by a 29–15 vote on March 15. The Whig leaders, Henry Clay and Daniel Webster, naturally cast their lot in opposition. But in another ironic twist to the Taney appointment, John C. Calhoun voted against his fellow southerner. For late in his judicial career, and for nearly a century afterward, Taney's reputation suffered as a result of his Dred Scott decision and its faithful support for Calhounian ideas of the nature of the union, sovereignty, and slavery.

While the Whigs despaired for the Court and the nation, the Democrats enjoyed their triumph. For over four decades, since the controversy over the Alien and Sedition Acts and Jefferson's clash with Marshall in the case of *Marbury* v. *Madison,* the federal judiciary had been a special target for Democratic scorn and invective. Jefferson's self-proclaimed heirs faithfully subscribed to his view that the Supreme Court was a Federalist refuge and a bastion for assault upon republican principles. Now the Democrats saw the Court as *theirs,* and they frankly welcomed the opportunity to alter traditional doctrines. Their leading journalist, William Leggett, particularly viewed Taney's appointment as both the symbolic and real instrument for change: "His [Taney's] republican notions, together with those of his present democratick associates, will produce a revolution in some important particulars in the doctrines heretofore advanced, . . . highly favourable to the independence of the States and the substantial freedom of the people." When Taney died in 1864, however, a dispassionate analysis of his career and opinions could certainly not identify him with any significant doctrinal "revolution." Indeed, Taney's judicial behavior largely vindicated John Marshall's earlier support of the Marylander.

With Taney presiding, the Supreme Court now contained five Jackson appointees. Only Story and Thompson remained from earlier days. In 1837 the justices' tenure averaged slightly more than eight years, and their average age only fifty-six. But despite the recent appointments, the Court's political coloration remained blurred. Jackson's earlier appointments of McLean and Baldwin could certainly not have made the Democrats feel too secure by 1837. McLean had thoroughly identified with the Whigs, and Baldwin had intimate ties to the hated Biddle bank in Philadelphia. The Jacksonian Democrats, like other political figures before and since, realized later the flimsy threads that bind a man's judicial role to his past political activities.

#   #   #

The changing membership of the Supreme Court coincided with a significant shift in the interpretation of corporate rights *vis-à-vis* the powers of government. The Dartmouth College decision in 1819, which held that a corporation charter is protected by the contract clause of the federal constitution, raised the question of what control, if any, legislatures retained over their creations. Fears that the decision would encourage rampant, unrestrained corporate power, were exaggerated however. Marshall's opinion did not wholly preclude the authority of the state to regulate corporate behavior when public interests so required. The framers of the Constitution, he said, "did not intend to restrain the states in the regulation of their civil institutions adopted for internal government." The essence of the Dartmouth College decision depended upon a charter or contract that restricted the future action of a state. It really had no application to legislative police regulations for the health, safety, or general welfare—those general aspects of sovereignty that cannot be bartered away. Furthermore, as Justice Story pointed out in his concurring opinion, states could reserve the power to alter or repeal charter provisions.

Story's observation was not startling. First, it was deeply rooted in republican ideas of checks and balances and limited legislative power. Jefferson, for example, had endorsed such ideas in the Virginia Statute of Religious Freedom of 1786. Although he placed religious freedoms within the context of irrevocable natural rights, Jefferson acknowledged that a legislature, "elected by the people for the ordinary purposes of legislation only, have no power to restrain the acts of succeeding assemblies, constituted with [equal] . . . powers." But theory and abstraction to the contrary notwithstanding, vested rights-oriented courts insisted upon a specific articulated reservation of power. For example, in 1806 the Massachusetts Supreme Court held in *Wales* v. *Stetson* that legally vested corporate rights could not be altered or destroyed by subsequent statutes unless the power for that purpose was reserved by the legislature in the act of incorporation.

Three years after *Wales* v. *Stetson,* the Massachusetts legislature passed a general act reserving the power to make further regulations of chartered corporations, or to repeal all or any part of a charter. Until the Dartmouth College case, the Massachusetts statute was unique though a few states had inserted repeal provisions in specific charters. As early as 1784 a Pennsylvania charter contained a reservation clause. Interestingly, despite the furor over the Dartmouth College decision, and the fears that it raised of "soulless monsters" dominating the people, the states responded rather haphazardly with general statutes or constitutional reservations of power. In 1826, the New York constitution provided for the passage of such an act, and the legislature enacted one the next year. Massachusetts altered its law in 1831, significantly after the Charles River Bridge case had gone through the state court. The Massachusetts law was a prototype for other states. It provided that all acts of incorporation passed thereafter, "shall at all times . . . be liable to be amended, altered, or repealed at the pleasure of the legislature," unless the grant contained an express limitation on the extent or duration of the reserved power. The charter could be repealed only when it had been violated by the grantee, or by some other default. In the same year that Massachusetts revised its general statute, the new Delaware constitution restricted legislative charter grants by requiring a two-thirds concurrence of the legislature in the grant and providing a reserved power of revocation for all charters. Also in 1831, Maine enacted a general statute similar to that of its sister state. But the neighboring state of New Hampshire passed no general law, and relied instead on an irregular pattern of inserting a reservation into individual charters. And New Jersey, a state already noted for its generosity toward corporations, did not enact a general reservation power until 1846. Ohio used a statute from 1842 until 1845. Its 1851 constitution provided for charter reservations but this was only after a six-year period in which numerous charters were granted, especially to banks, without such a stipulation. After the Dartmouth College case, most states attached a reservation clause to individual charters, but statutory or constitutional limitations were not generally introduced until the mid-1840s, or a quarter-century later.

The courts also moved to limit corporate charter rights by insisting upon very narrow and strict construction of charters in favor of the state. Again the 1806 Massachusetts case of *Wales* v. *Stetson* pointed the way. Chief Justice Theophilus Parsons had suggested then that statutes receive such a reasonable construction "as that the existing rights of the public, or of individuals, be not infringed." Appropriately enough, some decisions in the 1830s of the Marshall Court, and of Attorney General Taney, refined this idea so that it became a significant limitation, or qualification, to the Dartmouth College doctrine. Ultimately, it proved to be the basic legal reasoning for the disposition of the Charles River Bridge case.

A decade after the Dartmouth College case, the Marshall Court indicated its awareness of the conflicts between corporate powers and community needs. In a number of decisions the justices retreated from the broader perimeters established in earlier contract clause cases. In *Beaty* v. *Knowles* (1830) the Court announced a stricter construction of charter rights: "That a corporation is strictly limited to the exercise of those powers which are specifically conferred on it, will not be denied. The exercise of the corporate franchise being restrictive of individual rights, cannot be extended beyond the letter and spirit of the act of incorporation." The more important case of *Providence Bank* v. *Billings* came later the same year, and significantly with an opinion by Marshall. Taney relied heavily upon the Providence Bank case when the Supreme Court finally decided the bridge controversy, and accordingly it deserves careful examination.

Rhode Island chartered the Providence Bank in 1791. Thirty years later the legislature imposed a bank tax of fifty cents on every thousand dollars of capital stock. Later it raised the tax to $1.25. The Providence Bank stockholders, however, objected to the tax as unconstitutional because in effect it impaired the obligation of the contract created by the charter of incorporation. After an unsuccessful action of trespass against the bank's officers to prevent payment of the tax, the stockholders appealed to the United States Supreme Court.

Marshall wasted little time in exposing the flimsiness of the plaintiffs' argument and in marking out a new direction in contract interpretation. The original bank charter, he noted, contained no stipulation expressly exempting the bank from taxation. Eschewing any loose interpretation whatsoever, Marshall found nothing in the charter that indicated either of the parties intended a tax exemption. "The plaintiffs," Marshall said, "find great difficulty in showing that the charter contains a promise, either express or implied, not to tax the bank."

The bank claimed that unless the charter implied immunity, its rights and very existence were endangered. The syllogism was a neat one: taxation could absorb all profits, thus destroying the bank and consequently impairing the obligation of the contract. But Marshall flatly rejected the argument, calling it "extravagant." The Chief Justice, unlike Story in his later opinion in the Charles River Bridge case, refused to consider such a proposition in terms of "universal justice" or "abstract truth." It was not universal, he maintained, "and therefore its truth cannot be admitted, in these broad terms, in any case. We must look for the exemption in the language of the instrument; and if we do not find it there, it would be going far to insert it by construction." Considering a corporation *vis-à-vis* the state, Marshall noted that the object of incorporation was to grant the character and properties of individuality to a changing collective body. But Marshall insisted that privileges granted to the corporation exempting it from burdens common to individuals did not automatically flow from the charter; they must, he claimed, be expressed or they did not exist.

Marshall admitted that the tax could be excessive but denied that the federal courts could correct every abuse of power committed by the states. Although Marshall rarely is identified with the language of judicial restraint, he insisted here, like one of his successors, that for abuses against legislative power, the people must resort to the polls and not the courts. "The interest, wisdom, and justice of the representative body, and its relations with its constituents," Marshall observed, "furnish the only security where there is no express contract, against unjust and excessive taxation, as well as against unwise legislation generally."

Marshall emphasized the importance of protecting the integrity of the taxation power in the Providence Bank case. But this can be related to his more general concern for the powers of government — powers to enable it to serve the community's will and needs. The idea of effecting a balance between corporate rights and those of the community is more usually associated with Taney and judges other than Marshall. But when the vital powers of government were at stake, especially one so essential to the existence of government as taxation, Marshall too acknowledged the public interest. The whole community, he maintained, had an interest in retaining an undiminished taxation power, and therefore no court could presume its abandonment by the state unless the same had been expressly provided.* Marshall was here concerned that govern-

*Marshall and Taney both held that the power to tax could be alienated under such circumstances. See, for example, *New Jersey* v. *Wilson*, 7 Cranch 164 (1812), and *Piqua Branch of the State Bank* v. *Knoop*, 16 Howard 369 (1853).

ment not be unduly inhibited or restricted from changing policy. He recognized that government must retain its freedom to function and act in the future for the good of the community.

The Chief Justice had moved a considerable distance from his earlier position on strict contractual construction and taxation. In *New Jersey* v. *Wilson* (1812), perhaps Marshall's most extreme pro-private property decision, he held that a colonial tax exemption for Indian lands transferred to the new owners when the Indians sold their holdings to land speculators. The New Jersey Supreme Court had ruled that the colonial agreement was intended only for the Indians and could not be passed on without the state's consent. One of the state judges insisted that courts must never imply the surrender of the taxation power. Contracts binding future legislatures from raising taxes for the support of government and the needs of the community, he said, "ought at least to be clear and explicit, free from all doubt and uncertainty, not depending on implication and construction." But Marshall and his colleagues overruled the state court, and liberally construed the original immunity as applicable to all subsequent titleholders.

Marshall's narrow, strict construction of charter rights in favor of community considerations in the Providence Bank case is significant primarily in the light of future developments. Yet it should be understood in the larger context of his whole career. If Taney had written the same opinion, historians would see it as another manifestation of his concern for "community rights," and even more likely, as further evidence of his "states'-rights" proclivities. But John Marshall—the "supernationalist," the "conservative" with an excessive concern for "property rights,"—wrote the Providence Bank decision. To be sure, one opinion cannot negate or even undermine the main themes of Marshall's career. But then where does it fit into the whole meaning of his judicial behavior? Perhaps it best complements his basic and recurrent theme that government—*any* government immediately involved—must retain the energy and powers essential to governing so that the American people might avoid the specter of anarchy. John Marshall, child of the Revolution and the Confederation, never wavered in his struggle against anarchy and ineffective government, however imagined and unreal the threat.

Marshall's construction of the contract clause in the Providence Bank case in many respects was merely the other side of the same coin. It did not represent a sudden shift in goals. His earlier and better-known contract clause opinions were not idle abstractions that had the absolute protection of vested interests as the ultimate end. Instead, the protection of vested interests, particularly in the first three decades of the nineteenth century, was the most obvious and convenient means to secure desirable public goals.

Today the term "vested rights" has a negative and abstract connotation suggesting the dead hand of reaction; it further conveys a static conception of property and capital that belies the basic nineteenth century belief in a dynamic, expansive economy. Just as Marshall and Alexander Hamilton agreed on legal and constitutional principles, they had a common outlook regarding American economic development. It is not very new or profound to hold that Hamilton constructed a political-constitutional ideology as a means to an economic end; it would not be too much to credit Marshall with a similar purpose. Marshall offered ample evidence throughout his career that property rights had a larger community value and could on occasion be subordinated to the community's needs.

Certainly John Marshall, Chief Justice and an active land speculator, sought to protect certain categories of property, and certainly he reflected basic American beliefs. But what "we did in the name of vested rights," as Professor Willard Hurst has suggested, "had less to do with protecting holdings than it had to do with protecting ventures." The slogan of "vested rights" is altogether sterile; the protection of property interests involved rather practical considerations. As reflected in the American entrepreneurial mood and in Marshall's *Fletcher* v. *Peck* opinion, these were the protection of the innocent, bona fide investor, the realization that investment capital was scarce and must not be intimidated, and the consideration that the vast, undeveloped lands would remain an unrealized national treasure if a hostile legal or political milieu retarded capital investment.

In *Fletcher* v. *Peck,* Marshall satisfied himself that the land claimants had fulfilled the basic Lockean-Blackstonian requirement that their property be "justly earned." Whatever fraudulent conditions surrounded the land grants, the claimants were innocent, bona fide investors who need not suffer for the sins of others. Speaking of the plaintiff, Marshall held that the "concealed defect cannot be set up against him. He has paid his money for a title good at law; he is innocent, whatever may be the guilt of others, and equity will not subject him to the penalties attached to that guilt. All titles would be insecure, and the intercourse between man and man would be very seriously obstructed, if this principle be overturned." Rather than a static idealization of "vested rights," Marshall emphasized economic security—with peace and tranquility—primarily for the desirable end of encouraging *more* "intercourse between man and man."

The Providence Bank opinion abounds with such keen insights into our public policy that one wonders why it has attracted relatively little historical attention. Take, for example, Marshall's awareness of land distribution and the uses of taxation. He noted that land "has . . . been granted by government since the adoption of the constitution. This grant is a contract, the object of which is that the profits issuing from it shall enure to the benefit of the grantee. Yet the power of taxation may be carried so far as to absorb these profits. Does this impair the obligation of the contract? The idea is rejected by all." Here Marshall was doing far more than merely limiting a contract. He recognized the power and responsibility of the national government to use the distribution of land as a basis for economic growth. By insuring valid titles to the public domain, the government encouraged cultivation. Cleared and cultivated land was much more valuable to the national economy than the nominal sale price of $1.25 per acre, yet the government did not collect the difference. Instead, government used the difference as a subsidy to encourage the private sector of investment and to make the land a magnet to attract private capital. Settlement and economic expansion also offered the opportunity for state and local taxation, which in turn provided the means for such governmental services as roads, hospitals, asylums, and schools. Marshall's brief example, in short, summed up one way in which our public policy served the cause of national expansion, and a more humane and civilized society.

The Providence Bank decision received widespread approval. A conservative law review complained mildly that Marshall did not fully meet the questions involved and believed that the Court unfortunately had limited the wise ruling of the Dartmouth College case. But Whig journals, significantly enough, heartily approved of the decision. The *National Gazette,* for example, called it "particularly opportune and of a sound constitutional purport." Democratic newspapers naturally chimed in with support, thus strengthening the Court with both parties—a rare occurrence indeed.

The need for strict construction of charter and contract rights received further elaboration in a problem involving the monopoly privileges of a New Jersey railroad corporation. In 1832 the Camden & Amboy Railroad, and its junior partner, the Delaware and Raritan Canal Company, secured an act from the New Jersey legislature stipulating that the state would not incorporate any group to build a competing railroad between Philadelphia and New York. In exchange, the companies gave the state one thousand shares of stock and guaranteed the state a minimum of $30,000 per year in dividends and transit duties. In effect, New Jersey surrendered control of a large part of its railroad policy to a private monopoly, but under an arrangement that virtually promised to supply all necessary revenues to the state.

The Trenton and New Brunswick Turnpike Company, in which the Philadelphia and Trenton Railroad held a majority interest, sought permission in 1833 to build a rail line over the same route granted to the monopoly. The turnpike company's line of travel, as specified in its 1804 charter, paralleled part of that given to the monopoly. In support of their bill, the turnpike company secured favorable advisory opinions in 1833 and 1834 from Attorney General Taney and Chancellor James Kent of New York, with Daniel Webster endorsing the latter's opinion. The diverse approaches of Taney on the one hand, and Kent and Webster on the other, illustrate the fluid character of legal doctrine to achieve a desired public policy.

Taney's more elaborate opinion concerned itself with the right of one legislature to bind future ones. First, he saw the problem as one adversely affecting the rights of the community to secure needed improvements or, to phrase it differently, the power of the state to insure the proper conditions for the release of creative energy to serve the well-being and needs of the community. Then he invoked longstanding ideas of republican theory as the underpinning for his views on political economy. Taney denied that a state could contract away its power to act in behalf of the sovereign people. Specifically, the legislature could not deprive the state and the people of the power of "prosecuting such works of internal improvement as they deem necessary to advance their interests and promote . . . prosperity." Here then was the material reason for limiting legislative contracts, with the premium placed on economic and community growth. Taney further argued that it was "inconsistent with the spirit of our institutions, and dangerous to the best interests of the community" if a legislature could bind its successors. The effects could force "incurable" evils by inhibiting development; they could force people to forego their natural advantages and opportunities and thus "prevent them from using the means necessary to promote the prosperity and happiness of the community."

The Attorney General set his views of community development and economic growth within the framework and rhetoric of Revolutionary-Jeffersonian popular sovereignty theory. Legislatures, he noted, exercise only delegated powers and cannot bind the state beyond the scope of authority granted by the people. They are the "agent" of the sovereign people, and when they overstep their authority, their acts are void and not binding. The constituent, Taney said, "is not bound further than the agent is authorised to act for him." Finally, Taney contended that the tradition of frequent elections meant nothing if one legislature could so restrain the actions of its successors.

Chancellor Kent's opinion, while more narrowly legalistic, also recognized the public policy implications. Agreeing that the 1832 monopoly privilege was invalid, Kent relied on the fact that in 1804 the state had chartered a turnpike company that now wanted to build a railroad along its right-of-way to compete with the Camden & Amboy. The turnpike company, he found, had a pre-existing right, a "valid, subsisting, and unimpaired *right*." Kent chose not to discuss Taney's theoretical digressions; they were not, he said, necessary to his view of the case. He added, however, that "the legislative stipulation [of 1832] ought to be sternly construed, as one that may be exceedingly inconvenient to the public welfare." Thus Taney, the Jacksonian Democrat, and Kent, the unreconstructed Federalist, in their separate ways, realized that charter and contract privileges must neither imperil nor inconvenience the community and the public welfare.

Despite the learned opinions of such prominent authorities as Taney and Kent, the New Jersey legislature rejected the turnpike company's bill in 1835 and maintained the monopoly. The legislative decision reveals another dimension to the notion of community rights that did not need elaborate legal and political philosophies for support. Freedom, or at least substantial relief, from taxation was the preferred value of the New Jersey legislators and—apparently—their constituents. While Taney and Kent opted for growth and development, essentially a long-term proposition, the legislature preferred the short-term, but certain, advantages of tax relief as guaranteed by its arrangement with the railroad. Shortly after the affair, the Camden and Amboy gained the controlling interest in the Philadelphia and Trenton, thus ending a potential threat to its monopoly position. Significantly, the Camden and Amboy monopoly apparently feared litigation and realized that the legislature's essentially political decision had little chance against prevailing legal doctrine, whether of the Taney or Kent variety.

Marshall's and Kent's views on the construction of contracts and

charters wavered between sustaining corporate and individual interests and the larger interests of the community. But in the years
immediately preceding his appointment to the Supreme Court,
Taney held a consistent public position. In an 1832 opinion as attorney general he maintained that corporate charters and privileges were not designed for the exclusive benefit of the corporation. The privileges followed in order to secure a public convenience; the "interests of the public must," he insisted, "always be
regarded as the main object of every charter." Finally, in a private
opinion prepared for Jackson shortly after his confirmation as
Chief Justice, Taney reiterated his position on the interrelationship of corporate and community rights. He said that while every
charter contains special rights and privileges to the grantee, no
charter should grant rights and privileges only to advance the private interests of individuals. They must be granted in the expectation of promoting some public interest. He concluded that in making grants government must determine whether the charter "is
likely to produce any real benefit to the community, and whether
that benefit is sufficient to justify the grant."

#   #   #

The shifting views on public contracts and public policy, as ex-
emplified in the views of Taney, Marshall, and even Kent, reflected
various attempts to create a legal system that could meet the needs
of an enterprising, burgeoning society. Risk capital now was in
greater supply, and public policy and the resulting law adjusted
enough to encourage its utilization. This need not suggest that the
prerogatives of existing property, or even of properly vested rights,
were any less secure in 1837 than they were when John Marshall
spoke in the Dartmouth College case in 1819, or in *Fletcher* v. *Peck*
in 1810. But the demands of economic expansion were greater in
the 1830s than ever before. Technological innovations and improvements, such as railroads, were so crucial to continued and
rapid growth that in self-defense no community could allow entrenched privileges, or more especially, implied privileges, to inhibit or limit its freedom of action. The rights of certain individuals

and the needs of the larger group often conflict within a legal system. Legislatures and courts tried to make a utilitarian choice: they preferred whatever interest that brought the greatest good to the greatest number. Privileges that amounted to barriers and restraints on material gain and market exploitation would be sacrificed on the altar of progress. In the name of community rights, there would be no paralysis of governmental power to act in behalf of the community. This, at least, was the chief thrust of public policy doctrines favored by most Americans in the 1830s.

VI

RE-ARGUMENT, 1837

WHILE THE CHARLES RIVER BRIDGE CASE dragged on in Washington, the success of the Warren Bridge only increased the anxiety of the Charles River Bridge proprietors for compensation. By early 1832, the new bridge had earned enough to fulfill the conditions for making it a free avenue. Because the Warren Bridge proprietors feared the possibility of a court judgment imposing damages on their corporation, they persuaded the legislature to extend the tolls for another year. When the Supreme Court failed to act in 1833, the proprietors requested another extension. This time the state required the corporation to post bond that the excess tolls would be used only to sustain damages. Despite popular clamor for making the bridge free, the legislature renewed the tolls again in 1834 and 1835. Finally, on March 2, 1836, the bridge became free. Charlestown held a great celebration, but the gloom was thick in Cambridge. The dissolution of the Warren Bridge Corporation meant an end to its annuity payments to Harvard, and correspondingly, the Charles River Bridge proprietors refused to pay their portion. The college treasurer reported to the Harvard Corporation in September that the College's bridge shares "are at present valueless." Nevertheless, the Charles River Bridge remained open throughout 1836 and early 1837.

Surprisingly, the Charles River Bridge continued to attract more than one-third of the total tolls collected by the two bridges in the early 1830s. Net income remained below the pre-1828 levels of course, but the bridge continued to be profitable for longstanding investors. The state's attorney general reported the comparative earnings of the bridges to the state senate in 1835:

CHARLES RIVER BRIDGE

Years	Gross Receipts	Expenditures	Net Income
1832	$10,857.00	$4,315.15	$6,541.85
1833	12,389.00	4,952.72	7,436.28
1834	13,034.00	3,650.69	9,383.31

WARREN BRIDGE

1832	$21,806.00	$9,376.70	$12,429.30
1833	22,171.58	8,769.07	13,402.51
1834	21,850.90	5,423.44	16,427.46

#   #   #

The Supreme Court, newly reconstituted with Chief Justice Taney and the other Jacksonian appointees, assembled in Washington in January 1837. A Democratic publication, sensing the symbolism of change, proudly pointed to Taney as the first Chief Justice to wear the more "democratic" trousers instead of the knee breeches favored by his predecessors. The courtroom, then in the basement of the north wing of the Capitol, had been appropriately redecorated for the occasion. A popular Washington guidebook for 1837 described the setting as an "apartment" of a "semicircular shape, with the windows to the east to admit the light, which enters awkwardly and feebly, at the backs of the judges, on the bench. The arches in the ceiling diverge like the radii of a circle, from a point over the justice seat, to the circumference. On the wall is an emblem of justice, holding her scales, in bold relief, and also a figure of Fame, crowned with the rising sun, and pointing to the Constitution of the United States. The members of the bar are conveniently accommodated with seats and desks in the body of the apartment; and the visitors are furnished with rows of benches on the right and left wings of the centre of the court."

When the Court went into session on January 9, 1837, more than sixty cases were on the docket because of the persistent vacancies on the bench. Many, like the Charles River Bridge case, had been before the Court for over six years. Justice Wayne's absence delayed the bridge case arguments until January 19, after which they continued for six days. Public curiosity with the new members of the Court, and the appearance of Daniel Webster, attracted some interest to the arguments; the issues of the controversy, however, did not cause much of a stir in Washington. In any event, as Story reported to Charles Sumner, the audience was quite large—"a large circle of ladies, of the highest fashion, and taste, and intelligence, numerous lawyers, and gentlemen of both houses of Congress, and towards the close, the foreign ministers, or at least some two or three of them."

Webster and Warren Dutton still represented the Charles River Bridge proprietors. But new faces appeared for the defense. William Wirt, veteran of many significant constitutional law cases and chief counsel for the Warren Bridge group in 1831, had died in 1834, and the defendants decided to replace Walter Jones. In their place the Warren Bridge proprietors selected Massachusetts Senator John Davis, a Whig, and Simon Greenleaf, Royall Professor of Law at Harvard. Both men, prominent and esteemed in Massachusetts, surely lent added respectability to the defendants' cause. Greenleaf's appointment must also be regarded as a milestone in the history of academic freedom. Harvard College, after all, had a significant stake in an outcome favorable to the plaintiffs. When Greenleaf requested a leave of absence to represent the Warren Bridge, he realized there was no precedent for his request. The Law Department granted leaves for professional engagements only if they did not interfere with professorial obligations. The

Harvard Corporation, however, graciously voted permission for Greenleaf to argue the case in Washington.

Greenleaf was elected Royall Professor in 1833 upon the recommendation of Story. Born in Massachusetts in 1783, and educated in Newburyport, Greenleaf studied in a law office in New Gloucester, Maine. He moved to Portland in 1808 to practice law and soon established a preeminent reputation among the bar. When Maine became a state in 1820, the Maine Supreme Judicial Court selected him as its reporter, a position he held until his Harvard appointment. During that period he also served two terms in the legislature, where he helped to draft the state's legal codes. He attracted Story's attention in his practice before the United States Circuit Court in Portland, and through his reports and scholarly writing. Greenleaf's reports also impressed Chancellor Kent, who made much use of them in the preparation of his *Commentaries*. Greenleaf's professional and political fame in no way rivalled that of the other lawyers in the Charles River Bridge case. But as the arguments developed, he emerged as the dominant figure among the four.

The counsel and arguments on both sides deeply impressed Justice Story. He told Charles Sumner, then Greenleaf's temporary replacement at Harvard, that "it was a glorious exhibition for old Massachusetts." Story noted that his old friend, Webster, was in his best form, but allowed that Webster's closing reply had "too much of *fierté* here and there." Story generously and unqualifiedly praised Greenleaf's presentation, admitting "the force of his argument" although remaining unconvinced. "'Greek met Greek,'" he later told his son. In his dissenting opinion, Story again acknowledged the learning, research, and ability of the arguments; but here he significantly added that, in contrast to the 1831 arguments, the lawyers had based their cases on "varied and new grounds."

Webster and Dutton essentially relied upon the principles advocated in the state court and in the Supreme Court six years earlier. Confident in the justness of their cause, they pressed the legal verities that had served so well and so often in the past. Their briefs built upon certain basic assumptions. The Charles River

Bridge Corporation, they contended, had succeeded to the ferry rights held by Harvard College. The ferry had exclusive rights from one terminus to another, and the bridge naturally assumed the same advantage. The lawyers argued that this was the obvious and logical implication of the original bridge charter of 1785. The common law, English experience, and American precedents consistently supported a liberal construction of public charters granted for a valuable consideration. With this doctrine, Webster and Dutton maintained that the statute providing for the Warren Bridge had impaired and had violated the state's contractual obligations to the Charles River Bridge proprietors. They recognized that the new bridge did not directly destroy the old, but claimed that the indirect method had the same effect. A free bridge parallel to a toll bridge obviously doomed the latter. The tolls, Dutton said, "are of the essence of the grant—the very objects of it." If deprived of tolls, the franchise, for purposes of gain and profit, was worthless.

The plaintiffs' counsel insisted that courts must protect private property and interests from capricious and ephemeral legislative majorities. In particular, they urged the Supreme Court to continue "this most salutary and highest of all its functions [so that] the whole legislation of the country will be kept within its constitutional sphere of action." The "general confidence" and "general security" of the nation required no less, they concluded. In addition, they argued that public charters should be judicially construed. Courts should inquire as to what rights are created, and what covenants are implied, by public grants. In particular, Dutton contended, "every grant implies a covenant by the grantor *not to reassert his right over the thing granted.*" This notion was inherent in every public charter and, "as if written with *sympathetic ink,* not appearing till held up to the light of judicial interpretation."*

Dutton finally rested his case on the general need for security of property. If the state could destroy the Charles River Bridge, "*what* and *where* is the security for other corporate property," he

*This and other italicized expressions of counsel follow the form of Greenleaf's manuscript notes of the arguments.

asked. Dutton cleverly alluded to the most volatile investment issue when he noted that over four million dollars had already been
invested in state-chartered railroads. Those titles, he warned, were
no more secure than that of the bridge proprietors if the state pursued the same goal as it did with free bridges. Dutton scoffed at
defense contentions that property interests could be safely entrusted to the equity and justice of the legislature: "I answer all
such fine sentiments by holding up the charter of Charles River
bridge,' he retorted, "once worth half a million dollars; and now
not worth the parchment it is written upon."

Webster's rambling and bad temper marked his performance.
Perhaps he felt oppressed by the new judicial surroundings. Greenleaf had written Sumner that Webster was quite "uneasy and
moody" during the defense's presentation. At one point, Webster
told the defense counsel that he would tear their arguments to
pieces and abuse them. "The former will puzzle him," Greenleaf
confidently observed, and "the latter I doubt not he will do."

Webster denied that his clients stood in the way of progress and
improvements. But they were, he passionately believed, attempt-
ing to thwart a revolution against the foundations and security of
property. The plaintiffs opposed, said Webster, "the clamour
against legislative acts which have vested rights in individuals on
principles of equal justice to the state, and to those who hold those
rights under the provisions of the law." Webster basically reiterated
his familiar vested rights and contract clause arguments, and he
urged the Court to correct the legislature's abuse of power. The
Court, he said, should follow its own "enlightened conscience"
and unhesitatingly correct "improvident, inconsiderate, intemperate and hasty and sometimes ignorant legislation." But Webster,
depressed and sick at heart, knew before the decision that *this* court
would not have much of an "enlightened conscience," at least according to his lights. Webster had no illusions about the outcome.
More than a year earlier, when the Taney and Barbour appointments were pending, he told his colleague Dutton that their
"chances for justice" were slight. Soon after the opening of arguments, Webster wrote his son that he expected to lose the case.

Greenleaf's argument broke those "varied and new grounds" later acknowledged in Story's opinion. Apparently the respectable Harvard professor feared being identified with a radical cause. During the arguments he told Sumner that he and Davis had "avoided everything 'peoplish' in our remarks, confining ourselves to legal views alone." Nevertheless, such criticism must have developed. When Greenleaf filed his case materials in the Harvard Law Library after the conclusion of the case, he added a covering note expressing dismay that some persons had misrepresented his argument, as though, he said, "it was agrarian in character, & tended to the destruction of vested rights, & justified the taking of private property for public uses *without* compensation." He insisted then, as he did throughout the case, that he had placed the defense "on the acknowledged principles of constitutional and common law."

Greenleaf and Davis opened their arguments by calling attention to the "insuperable difficulties" standing in the way of a decree in favor of the plaintiffs. The defendants, they noted, no longer had control of the Warren Bridge because title had passed to the state as provided for in their charter. Then, responding to the specific allegations of the Charles River Bridge proprietors, the defense counsel countered that the ferry always had been subject to the control of the state; that it had never passed to the plaintiffs, but was resumed by the state after compensating the college; and that neither the ferry grant nor the bridge grant contained any exclusive privileges prohibiting the state from opening a new bridge. They offered an alternative line of principles and precedents refuting the plaintiffs' insistence upon a liberal construction of public charters. Further, if the Charles River Bridge proprietors had sustained losses as a result of the competing bridge, the damages were merely consequential. There could be no remedy lying against the defendants for they no longer held title in the new bridge. The plaintiffs could only seek relief from the state, but following that course, they would have to rely upon the legislature's "liberality".

Greenleaf's allegedly novel arguments involved the powers of the state and eminent domain. Even conceding all the presumed

and implied privileges claimed by the plaintiffs, the charter nevertheless would be void. The legislature, he maintained, had no authority to surrender its right of eminent domain and thereby impair the community's effectiveness to secure public improvements.
The power of eminent domain, he continued, was entrusted to legislatures for the perpetual benefit of the public and could not be
bartered away. The Charles River Bridge proprietors had received
their original charter subject to the limitation of eminent domain.
The power was inherent, "as if written in *sympathetic ink*, in *every
public contract.*" In addition, Greenleaf argued that when the
Charles River Bridge proprietors accepted an extension of their
charter in 1792, they thereby acknowledged the state's right to
make new and competing grants at its discretion.

Greenleaf presented a host of English and American precedents
justifying the strict construction of public charters. The basic principle, he suggested, was that where the grantee claims anything of
power or privilege, entrusted to the crown or legislature for purposes of governing or for the general good, the grant must be
"sternly construed, as one that may be exceedingly inconvenient
to the public welfare." In short, when the community's well-being
or progress were at stake, nothing in a charter could pass by implication. On this principle, Greenleaf suggested, the plaintiffs'
charter gave them a franchise coextensive with the bridge itself,
but nothing else. That is, the state only authorized the corporation
to erect a bridge in the place designated, and to take certain tolls.
Greenleaf noted incidentally, that the Supreme Court never had
held a state law void for violating an *implied* contract. On the contrary, in recent cases heard by John Marshall and his colleagues,
such as the Providence Bank case, the Court had refused to imply
conditions or privileges in public contracts. Unlike his colleagues
who had argued the case in the state court, Greenleaf could invoke
the words of the venerated Marshall. It must have been a trying
moment for Daniel Webster.

Greenleaf stressed the pernicious consequences of liberal construction of state-granted franchises, seeing it as inhibiting public
necessity and the corresponding obligation and power of govern-

ment to act in behalf of the community. If the state conceded such privileges, he warned, the Charles River Bridge would be a barrier to convenience and progress. The area was growing, the population expanding; but the plaintiffs insisted upon the maintenance of only one conveyance, a conveyance designed for the public's needs of a half century earlier. "To support pretensions so extravagant," he said, "well may they resort to the doctrines of the feudal system—for the claim is a monopoly in its most odious form." The defense also shrewdly justified strict construction as a convenient tool for courts. Strict construction, they noted, skirted the dilemma posed by the Hobson's choice of subjecting charter rights to the mercy of the state or, on the other hand, making the public subject to any and all extravagant claims of corporations.

Greenleaf generally eschewed the popular rhetoric against monopolies. Instead, he pitched his argument to the powers and duties of government. Sovereign power, he said, resides in the people, who in turn delegate the use of some power to their representatives and functionaries. None of this power can be bargained away by a legislature; each legislative body, on the other hand, assembles with the same authority vested in its predecessors. The sovereign people temporarily endow each legislature with the right of eminent domain to use in behalf of the community. That power, Greenleaf maintained, is inalienable, and any act of the legislature, "disabling itself from the future exercise of its trust for the public good, is void." As an example, he suggested that a legislature could not make a grant of land carrying with it a covenant forever excluding the construction of a fortress on the land for public defense. Following Vattel on public law, Greenleaf argued that the right of eminent domain, like the powers of taxation and of providing for the common defense in time of war, could not be alienated or impaired; it was, he concluded, "essential to the existence of all government whatever."

Greenleaf warned that the plaintiffs' claims threatened the government's obligation to provide internal improvements and generally advance the public welfare. He drew a direct connection between such power and economic growth. If the state had covenanted with new railroads to the effect that no more grants would be made, then "*all* future travel out of the state by any other routes would be at an end; — & the *very power* to grant new roads *of any sort* would *be annihilated!*" Interestingly, Greenleaf had a copy of Taney's 1833 opinion in the Camden and Amboy Railroad case, and though he did not cite it directly, he certainly exploited its doctrines and assumptions.

The issues were thus reduced to how and who would determine public policy for the community. Greenleaf insisted that roads and bridges were essential to the governing of the state: the people must be defended and they must have facilities for common travel from place to place. There was not, for example, a similar necessity for banks. Roads are necessary and useful. Banks are useful, but expedient; they are not, Greenleaf said, "essential to the constitution of civil society." Legislative powers must always be able to secure and satisfy public necessities, and therefore no legislature could abridge or limit the future exercise of the powers required to fulfill public wants.

Greenleaf sharply disputed the plaintiffs' contention that exclusive privileges were necessary to protect and foster enterprise. He responded that limitations on public grants would beneficially restrain speculative gambling, with all its deleterious side-effects. He also believed that legislatures would wisely protect corporations by withholding rival charters. Furthermore, chancery courts could restrain private competition by injunction. Exclusive grants were unnecessary, he insisted; "only agree to remunerate them, & men enough will be found to venture." His colleague, Senator Davis, also noted that while the suit had been pending for years, and judgment had been given against the plaintiffs, the spirit of enterprise was never higher in Massachusetts. Following Justice Morton's comment in the state court decision, Greenleaf twitted the Charles River Bridge proprietors for their "own mistake" and "want of prudence" in not having secured a more explicit charter.

Finally, Greenleaf closed with a plea for judicial restraint and respect for the state's willingness to meet her obligations. He reiterated his belief that Massachusetts' conduct had "been uniformly dignified, honorable & just." If not, and if the plaintiffs deserved a remedy, the state would "readily submit" to the Court's decree. Greenleaf and Davis maintained throughout that the old bridge proprietors' damages were "merely consequential." Their condition and claim was no different from that of others who suffered from public improvements. Davis noted that railroads for example, generally displaced nearby highways, rendering consequent losses to stages, wagons, and contiguous highway properties; but there was no indemnity for such losses. He labelled such losses a "mere misfortune," and added that the affected parties could have no right over, or interest in, the public travel that might be the subject of a legal claim. "The public convenience demands such improvements," he continued, "and they are not to be obstructed from such causes." If the plaintiffs were "merely sufferers," Greenleaf added, "either by the ordinary changes in human affairs, or by the legitimate exercise of . . . eminent domain," then he urged the Court to allow the state to settle the affair with "a just regard to its honor."

#   #   #

Less than three weeks after the conclusion of arguments, the Court reached its decision. "You have triumphed," Justice Story wrote to Greenleaf, as the new Jacksonian majority resolved nearly nine years of litigation. Chief Justice Taney, along with three other Jackson appointees, Baldwin, Wayne, and Barbour, affirmed the state court decision and held for the Warren Bridge. McLean voted to dismiss the case for lack of jurisdiction, although he clearly favored the claims of the Charles River Bridge proprietors. Story and Thompson, the only pre-Jackson members of the Court, dissented.

VII

THE NEW DISPENSATION AND THE LAST OF THE OLD RACE

THE SUPREME COURT'S decision in 1837 involved a full-scale debate between Chief Justice Taney and Justice Story on the substantive issues, the nature of public policy, and the judicial function. The clash marked an institutional watershed. After John Marshall became Chief Justice in 1801, he introduced the custom of a single opinion by the justices in contrast to the earlier practice of delivering opinions *seriatim.* To be sure, there were occasional dissents in the Marshall years, and the Chief Justice often trimmed his views in order to secure unanimity. But by 1837, the justices' political genealogy spanned three decades, which in turn reinforced the diversity of their views. The Charles River Bridge case may well mark the origins of dissent over basic values within the Supreme Court. At no time prior to 1837 had the disagreement in a major case been so sharp and fundamental. The Charles River Bridge decision thus demolished the illusion of consensus within the judiciary, just as certainly as the Bank War had exposed it within other political, social, and economic spheres of American life.

# # #

Chief Justice Taney's opinion for the Court combined specific legal principles with emerging general concepts involving the role of government and the public interest. He applied these specific principles and general concepts in order to serve particular purposes of the society and the economy. He utilized the law as a handmaiden for change, progress, and growth. As a speciman of judicial craftsmanship, Taney's opinion was of the highest caliber, dexterously joining *stare decisis* to a recognition of changes in American life that demanded legal accommodation. Actually, Taney offered little that was doctrinally new. He fashioned his views from early state court decisions, an English precedent, opinions by John Marshall and his colleagues, and the arguments of counsel. Taney's opinion marked not the emergence of a new idea, but rather the triumph of a competing idea, now propelled by a decisive political—and judicial—majority.

However much political considerations may have influenced Taney's opinion, it is worth noting that his remarks were almost devoid of Jacksonian rhetoric. Indeed, it may not be stretching the point too far to suggest that John Marshall could have written the same opinion. But Taney's views of economic progress, technological change, and the interwoven responsibilities of government were not uniquely his or those of a "Jacksonian Democrat." Marshall, the anachronistic Virginia Federalist, and Taney, the Maryland Democrat, who only recently and reluctantly had shed his Federalist label, simply were not very far apart on these problems in the 1830s.

At the outset, Taney acknowledged that the case presented questions of the "gravest character." He also noted that great pecuniary interests were at stake and, as in most legal choices, all sides would be affected, and someone harmed. Taney phrased the choices a bit more abstractly: the Court, he said, must guard "the rights of property, and at the same time carefully . . . [abstain] from any encroachment on the rights reserved to the States." It should be emphasized that Taney's conception of state rights in no way corresponds to the modern, and essentially negativist, connotation of the term. As evidenced by the whole of his opinion, Taney had clearly in mind an active and positive view of state *powers*.

The Chief Justice reduced the plaintiffs' argument to two basic propositions. First, the 1650 grant to Harvard entitled the college to a perpetual and exclusive right to operate a ferry between Charlestown and Boston. Massachusetts, in turn, transferred and vested those rights in the Charles River Bridge proprietors, thus giving the latter exclusive rights in the line of travel. Second, and independent of the ferry rights, the proprietors claimed that the acts of 1785 and 1792 "necessarily implied" that the legislature would not authorize a competing bridge. In any event, the original charter was a contract and the grant to the Warren Bridge group thus impaired the obligation of the contract. But Taney, after summarizing the position of the proprietors, immediately indicated that nothing would pass by implication. The plaintiffs, he said, must "show that the State had entered into a contract with them . . . not to establish a free bridge. . . . Such, and such only, are the principles upon which the plaintiffs . . . can claim relief."

Taney declared quite simply that the ferry rights were non-existent; therefore the proprietors had no claim to them whatsoever. The bridge itself, he maintained, had destroyed the ferry when it took its place and assumed its same functions. With the ferry destroyed, how could rights incidental to it have survived? Whatever exclusive privileges attached to the ferry followed the fate of the ferry. "The privilege of exclusion could not remain in the hands of [the] . . . assignees," Taney said, "if those assignees destroyed the ferry."

Taney could not resist the irony of the proprietors' claims to Harvard's privileges. The state had chartered the Charles River Bridge because of public need when the ferry proved inadequate. When the prospective proprietors petitioned the legislature in 1785, they had ignored Harvard's claims and stressed the greater demands of public interest and convenience and the superior advantages of a bridge over a ferry. The legislature had in turn accepted and then acted upon these principles. The bridge charter was not dependent upon Harvard's consent. The legislature, with the acquiescence of the proprietors, treated the subject as wholly within its power and ignored any claims of exclusive rights. In short, it considered the ferry rights extinguished by the bridge grant. The legislature compensated the college for the loss of its ferry operation, but nothing in the legislative documents in 1785, or thereafter, indicated an intent to reserve or later continue the ferry rights. The ferry, Taney concluded, "with all its privileges was intended to be forever at an end." In effect, the Chief Justice contended that the state had resumed the ferry privilege in order to construct a bridge in its place.

Taney concluded his discussion of the ferry rights by insisting upon a narrow construction of the charter. "The charter to the bridge is a written instrument which must speak for itself, and be interpreted by its own terms." Nothing in the charter associated the rights of the college with the bridge proprietors, and Taney noted that there was "no rule of legal interpretation" which authorized the Court even to infer such an association. This narrow construction was the theoretical basis for Taney's whole point of view in the case. And just as he used it to dispose of the question of the continuity of ferry rights, so he employed it to reject the proprietors' contention that the charter "necessarily implied" an exclusive control over the line of travel to the Charles River Bridge Company.

Throughout his opinion Taney confidently asserted that the "rule" of narrow construction in cases that involved the public interest was well-settled. For particular support he relied on an English case and recent Marshall Court decisions. Interestingly enough, the English case, *Stourbridge Canal* v. *Wheeley,* proved as useful to Story in his dissent as it did to the Chief Justice. Taney, however, noted that the English court considered the established rule of construction as one resolving any ambiguity in a public contract in favor of the public, and that the grantees could "claim nothing that is not clearly given them in the act." The facts and issues of the English case were not at all analogous to the bridge controversy. It involved an attempt by canal proprietors to charge tolls for use of their waterways when boats did not pass through the company's locks. The court held that the charter did not authorize such charges, either specifically or by clear "inference" from some of its provisions. Taney exploited the court's doctrine of strict construction, whereas Story grasped the English judge's acknowledgement of resulting rights when they could be clearly implied.*

A common ploy of a Supreme Court justice is to use the decisions and language of a distinguished predecessor to make a different goal more palatable to the public or to his colleagues. In the 1920s Chief Justice William Howard Taft consistently qualified the traditional doctrine that production could not be regulated under the interstate commerce power of the federal government. Chief Justice Charles Evans Hughes, in 1937, approvingly quoted Taft's *dicta* in order to overthrow completely the same doctrine and open the path for massive federal regulation of the economy. To offset the vigorous protest within his own court and the outraged cries of a large part of the legal and business community, Hughes deftly utilized the language of Taft, that impeccable constitutionalist.

Similarly, in 1837, Chief Justice Taney shrewdly invoked the decisions of his predecessor, the most important of which was Marshall's Providence Bank opinion of 1830. Taney insisted that the state action in the Charles River Bridge case was analogous to Rhode Island's bank tax. The proprietors' arguments were the

*The Stourbridge Canal case was an action of assumpsit brought by the canal proprietors against coal transporters who had refused to pay tolls. The parliamentary act chartering the canal provided that the proprietors could charge tolls for passage through any of the canal's locks. The defendants, however, had used a collateral cut of the Stourbridge, containing no locks, to link up to another canal. The proprietors maintained that only those who passed through the locks, and therefore paid tolls, were entitled to navigate the canal or any of its cuts. The defendants insisted that the canal was a public utility and that all persons were eligible to use it, paying rates only when properly authorized. The judge framed the conflict within the question of charter construction. For charters of public utility, he contended that the rule of strict construction was fully established: "that any ambiguity in the terms of the contract must operate against the adventurers, and in favor of the public; and the plaintiffs can claim nothing which is not *clearly* given them by the act." All this, of course, was most useful for Taney. But after the English judge found that the plaintiffs had no express right to receive compensation except for passage through the locks, he was willing for them to demonstrate "a right *clearly* given by inference" from other clauses of the charter. The implications, however, were not apparent enough and the judge held that the company could impose no burdens on the canal users, for its own benefit, except those clearly specified in the charter. *The Proprietors of the Stourbridge Canal against Wheely and others* (2 Barn. & Ald. 792).

same as those of the bank; that is, the state's power, if it existed, could destroy the franchise it had granted. But Taney, like Marshall, treated this only as a consequential, or incidental, effect. That the power might be exercised so as to destroy the franchise could not, he concluded, "in any degree affect the principle."

In the Providence Bank case, Marshall had been concerned with the power of taxation, a power basic and crucial for the existence of government. Taney, however, raised Marshall's use of a specific power to a general proposition involving the total power and purpose of government. The power to tax is essential if government is to function in behalf of the whole community. But Taney saw taxation as only one means to a larger end, and the power to serve such ends could not be diminished: "[T]he object and end of all government," he insisted, "is to promote the happiness and prosperity of the community by which it is established; and it can never be assumed, that the government intended to diminish its power of accomplishing the end for which it was created." Taney shrewdly perceived the vital role of government in stimulating the release of energy needed to serve and satisfy the requirements of a growing, free, active, and enterprising nation. Specifically, new channels of communication—"safe, convenient, and cheap"—were needed to maintain such activity; they served both travel and trade and were "essential to the comfort, convenience, and prosperity of the people." No government, Taney reiterated, could presume to surrender its power to provide for or encourage the development of these channels of communication. As with the power of taxation, "the whole community have an interest in preserving it undiminished."

Nothing more infuriated, or perhaps embarrassed, Taney's Whig detractors than his use of Marshall to complement and secure what some of them saw as exclusively Jacksonian rhetoric and doctrine. They insisted, for example, that the cases were not analogous; the taxation in the bank case did not indicate a certain tendency and intent to destroy the institution as did the chartering of the Warren Bridge. The chief criticism came down to a conflict as old as government itself. The purpose of government is to maintain an ordered community so as to better insure the freedom and happiness of its individual constituents. But to what extent may government diminish or harm the rights and well-being of any individual, or group of individuals, in order that the community at large may benefit?

One Whig critic flatly maintained that "government becomes subversive of its own end, when its purpose is bent to destruction." Marshall, he contended, never sanctioned governmental power or action that was confiscatory in its result. Anticipating this line, Taney refused to distinguish the power to tax from "any other affecting the public interest." The principles were the same, he said, and the rule of charter construction must be the same. Turning to the Massachusetts case, Taney argued that the "interests" of a large part of the community were unquestionably affected if the state should surrender control of a line of travel, for profit, to a corporation for its exclusive operation during seventy years. Taney paid his respects to individual rights—and there is no reason to doubt his commitment—but he emphasized their qualified character: "While the rights of private property are sacredly guarded, we must not forget that the community also have rights, and that the happiness and well being of every citizen depends on their faithful preservation."

The argument was complementary: on one hand, the community benefits when it maintains individual rights; but individual rights must, of necessity, sometimes bow to the needs and well-being of the community. The resolution, then as always, was a practical one, and here Taney saw the "rights" of the community as paramount. Summing up his views of "positive" government and community rights, the Chief Justice neatly combined older Federalist notions with the leaven of Jacksonian rhetoric: "The continued existence of a government would be of no great value, if by implications and presumptions, it was disarmed of the powers necessary to accomplish the ends of its creations; and the functions it was designed to perform, transferred to the hands of privileged corporations." In effect Taney recognized the existence of both focused interests or claims, and the framework or supporting in-

terests necessary for an effective existence and pursuit of the specific ones. His decision was practical because it acknowledged the
necessity for maintaining the functions and needs of social organization or social infrastructure, on which the more particular activities and relations depend.

Firmly establishing the principles of narrow construction and
the inviolability of certain governmental functions, Taney proceeded to refute the claims of the Charles River Bridge proprietors.
Their charter provided no exclusive privileges over the river, no
right to erect another bridge for themselves, or to prevent others
from doing so. Furthermore, the charter did not expressly pro-
hibit the state from building another bridge. The plaintiffs could
only infer such conditions, and in this case, obviously nothing would
pass by implication. Taney also cited the charter of the West Boston
Bridge in 1792 to prove that the state had not intended to deprive
itself of making further improvements over the river. When the
state extended the Charles River Bridge charter at the same time,
Taney noted that the legislature's language carefully avoided any
implication that the extension amounted to a compromise or compensation.

Taney's opinion, however, was somewhat ambiguous as to
whether the state could ever specifically surrender, even for a limited period of time, its power to make improvements or any other
power basic to the "happiness and prosperity" of the community.
He recognized throughout, as he did in similar opinions as attorney general, that government could grant certain privileges to
individuals who embarked on enterprises of value to the community. Furthermore, while he specifically acknowledged that the
state's power of "promoting the comfort and convenience" of the
people could not be surrendered or diminished, he added, as a
qualification, "unless it shall appear by plain words that it was intended to be done." Taney's language in the Charles River Bridge
case, and his decisions in future cases, clearly illustrate that the
contract clause of the federal constitution still had force. The chief
limitation was that nothing could be implied when the public interest was at stake. This limitation, incidentally, is related to Taney's
conception of the judicial function. To infer from a contract things

that a legislature had presumably avoided implying with great care, would constitute an excess of judicial power, acting upon its own prejudices with "a sort of judicial coercion." The proprietors' alleged privilege of exclusivity for bridge transportation would have vitally affected a broad array of interests. Accordingly, such an impact required a clear decision for such a right from the broadly-represented lawmaking body. Courts had much less claim to such representativeness than legislatures and Taney properly hesitated to sustain implicatory claims.

The touchstone of Taney's opinion was its practicality, its responsiveness to contemporary reality — in short, it was a document of public policy. The material progress of society, Taney observed, is prompted by technological change and improvement. Law should be a spur, not an impediment. It should allow for some loss, some sacrifice in order to make way for the new. In the past, successive turnpikes followed the same routes; then, in some cases, railroads ruined the turnpike corporations. New techniques provide the *raison d'être* for internal improvements. If the Charles River Bridge proprietors carried their point, Taney rightly feared that the courts would face all sorts of suits. He envisioned, for example, turnpike corporations "awakening from their sleep and calling upon this court to put down the improvements which have taken their place." Property and capital invested in railroads and canals would be jeopardized; more than that, venture capital would be discouraged. The prospects were grim, Taney noted: "We shall be thrown back to the improvements of the last century, and obliged to stand still, until the claims of the old turnpike corporations shall be satisfied, and they shall consent to permit these States to avail themselves of the lights of modern science, and to partake of the benefit of those improvements which are now adding to the wealth and prosperity, and the convenience and comfort of every other part of the civilized world." The Supreme Court, he concluded, would not "sanction principles which must lead to such results." Taney cast the law with the new entrepreneurs, the present rather than the past risk-takers, as the preferred agents for material progress. Only thus could technological advances be applied rapidly. One writer has put it more bluntly: Justice Story and those who supported the Charles River Bridge stood for the "horse and buggy," while Taney cleared the path for the "onrushing railroad."

Given the materialistic drives and dreams of the Americans—a people "forever moving on"—the Taney arguments made sense. He allied our laws with broadened entrepreneurial opportunity, even at the expense of past commitments of assets. Americans in the nineteenth century faced a land of rich and boundless opportunities for material reward. Nothing so threatened the aspirations of nineteenth century Americans as the scarcity of capital; nothing, therefore, required greater legal encouragement than venture capital, subject to the normal risks and vicissitudes of the market. It was this that took a local dispute over a free bridge out of its provincial setting and thrust it into the larger debate over political economy. Retrospectively, in a century that put a premium on "progress," and the release of creative human energy to propel that progress, the decision was inevitable.

Taney's Charles River Bridge opinion helped free new forms of property from the impeding, sometimes aggressive claims of obsolescent corporations that desperately tried to preserve exclusive earning opportunities. Such corporations often had vague and ambiguous charters, and represented the kind of abstraction cited by Taney in his example of turnpike roads and railroads. The plaintiff's claims in the Maryland case of *The Washington and Baltimore Turnpike Co.* v. *The Baltimore and Ohio Railroad* two years afterwards vindicated Taney's fears. The title of the case neatly summed up the issues. A Maryland turnpike company, chartered in 1812, brought an action of trespass against the railroad for building its route between the two cities and connected by the turnpike's line of travel. The railroad had done so under authority of four charters granted by Maryland between 1827 and 1833. The turnpike company charged that the railroad charters impaired its contract, threatened its existence, and so amounted to a deprivation of property without compensation. The situation paralleled that of the Charles River Bridge in that the new competition was destructive of an existing (although physically different) property form. A Maryland county court ignored the turnpike company's claim and found for the railroad. The Maryland high court subsequently affirmed the decision without opinion. Cognizant of community desires for the obvious advantages of the railroad, the courts refused to intervene in behalf of the extravagantly obstructionist claims of established competing interests.

As a problem of public policy, the Charles River Bridge decision was the practical one in terms of broad public policy needs. Still, "legal doctrine" needed some support, and Taney found such support in the tool of strict construction. This enabled him to work out the balance between competing private interests and community needs. Despite the Chief Justice's rough handling of the proprietor's claims, his dictum that the "rights of private property must be sacredly guarded" was not an empty one on his part. He neither denied Webster's argument, nor refuted Story's opinion, that investors would be discouraged if they found their property insecure every time the state or community desired a change. If titles were valid, if charter rights and privileges were explicit, Taney never would have approved their arbitrary destruction. In such cases, Taney and his judicial contemporaries, federal and state, insisted upon the implementation of eminent domain, that is, the taking of private property for public use but with compensation to the owners. Eminent domain is an equitable resolution of the constant tension between the demands of the community and the prerogatives of private property, and as the rate of technological innovation increased and new communities developed in the nineteenth century, it was increasingly employed. It applied, however, only in cases of indisputable rights and prerogatives of ownership. In cases such as the Charles River Bridge, courts have dismissed eminent domain as irrelevant, as Taney did in his one reference to it. Compensation here depended solely upon the beneficence of the state. But in no manner was the Charles River Bridge case a requiem for private property in the United States.

#   #   #

The Charles River Bridge decision was a crushing blow to Justice Story. "A case of grosser injustice, or more oppressive legislation, never existed," he wrote to his wife. "I feel humiliated, as I

think every one here is, by the Act which has now been confirmed."
Story, his judicial world collapsing about him, despaired for the
Court and the nation. Soon after the decision, he talked about re-
signing, but McLean and others dissuaded him. Webster, of course,
remained loyal and admiring. He told Story that his opinion was
the "ablest, and best written" he had ever delivered. But Webster,
too, was melancholy about the future: "The intelligent part of the
profession will all be with you," Webster said. "There is no doubt
of that; but then the decision of the Court will have completely
overturned, in my judgment, one great provision of the Constitution." Story felt keenly the loss of past values. "I am the last of the
old race of judges," he lamented to Harriet Martineau. "I stand
their solitary representative, with a pained heart, and a subdued
confidence."

Story's opinion was substantially the one he had prepared in
1831, tailored somewhat to respond to Taney. The thrust, however, was the same. In 1831, when the Court divided, Story revealed that the conflict revolved around the problem of strict
construction of charters. Then and later he believed that three
centuries of law and practice, English and American, favored a
liberal construction in behalf of grantees. The confrontation between Taney and Story thus resulted in a debate over economic
theory and the purposes of public policy. Story's massive documentation of the common law, along with English and American
precedents, probably gave him the better of the doctrinal contest—or in what Story himself called the "old law." But Story
bucked a powerful tide of opinion and was wholly out of line with
the prevailing commercial ethos. Yet with a tenacity born of deep-
rooted conviction, with an adherence to older and more experi-
enced values, and with a sense of history, Story pursued his cause
in spite of his isolation.

At the outset of his opinion, Story challenged the Chief Justice's
version of charter construction. The original Charles River Bridge
charter, he argued, dictated a liberal construction. He correctly
observed that the charter was vague as to the obvious purpose and
intent. The act nowhere really conferred an authority upon the

corporation to build a bridge, except by "inference and implication" from the preamble. For Story, this was "irresistible proof"
that the court must resort "to the common principles of interpretation, and imply and presume things, which the legislature has not
expressly declared." In a real sense, Story tried to preserve a judicial role in the interpretation of charters. He recognized a certain
sterility, a kind of built-in judicial obsolescence, in Taney's conception of strict construction. If courts and judges were not at
liberty to presume and imply meanings of charters, there would
be, he said, an end to the case. From this, Story launched a long
explanation and support for what he considered the proper rules
of interpretation.

Story's opinion was a veritable treatise. Extensively researched,
it offered a parade of precedents, all marshaled in an imposing
array to support the most extravagant claims for entrepreneurial
privilege. Story metaphorically worshipped at the altar of the common law, indulging in constant references to, for example, the
"doctrine of my Lord Coke, and of the venerable sages of the law
in other times."

Story contended that the Charles River Bridge grant was one of
contract, and not of bounty. In exchange for the grant, the proprietors had offered a valuable consideration to the state, that is,
a satisfaction of public need and convenience that would encourage
enterprise and commerce. He compared this to a royal grant in
which the king received some consideration, as opposed to one of
mere donation flowing from the bounty of the crown. The latter,
he acknowledged, allowed a construction wholly in the king's favor. But in cases where valuable consideration was received, the
grant was the same as any private one and was to be construed in
favor of the grantee. "It would be to the dishonour of the government," Story said, "that it should pocket a fair consideration, and
then quibble as to the obscurities and implications of its own contract." Republican justice, he added, should be no less than that
of monarchy.

In classical Whig fashion, Story polarized the conflict as a simple
one between lawful vested rights on the one hand, and arbitrary

capricious prerogative on the other. He thought this indulgence of American legislative prerogative infinitely worse than the greatest excesses of Tudor and Stuart monarchs. For him, the battles against despotism were over and the lessons and principles clear. "I stand upon the old law; upon law established more than three centuries ago, in cases contested with as much ability and learning as any in the annals of our jurisprudence, in resisting any such encroachments upon the rights and liberties of the citizens, secured by public grants. I will not," he vowed, "consent to shake their title deeds by any speculative niceties or novelties." Story's target here, of course, was Taney's doctrine of community rights and interest. So it is not surprising that despite his massive documentation, Story ignored the Marshall Court decisions that sustained such a view, decisions to which Story had at the time acquiesced. Story profoundly disliked the "new" doctrine and betrayed his impatience with the voguish premium on "progress." He insisted that the grant be examined within its original context. The risks had been great when the state had approved the venture. Economic conditions in the 1780s were not exactly propitious and the risk was further increased by the political instability that obtained under the Confederation. In addition, the very idea was technically hazardous; no one rightly knew for certain that the bridge could be built. Story emphasized these facts in order to refute any notion that the legislature had been deceived into an unwise grant, or that the proprietors' prospective rewards were out of proportion to their immediate perils. If the whole venture failed, the proprietors alone assumed the loss; the community's risk was nil and the public stood only to gain. The grant was only "in furtherance, and not in derogation of the public good."

Story believed that "natural" law and the "first principles of justice" forbade the legislature from doing indirectly what it could not do directly. From that, his conclusions fell neatly into line. He cited the decision in *Fletcher* v. *Peck* to deny that a legislature could revoke its own grant. Furthermore, he maintained that when a state granted privilege, it implicitly gave whatever was necessary for taking and enjoying it. In the case of the Charles River Bridge,

the unimpaired taking of tolls was indispensable for the full enjoyment of the proprietors' rights to conduct their transport facility. If denied the tolls, directly or indirectly, the franchise was
worthless. It was this right that was exclusive and to deny it was,
in effect, to impair the obligation of the contract. The rights over
the whole river, he added, need not be exclusive. He believed that
the grant implied an exclusive franchise to a reasonable distance
so that the owners would not be injured by competition. He thus
applied the common law of ferry rights to bridges: "Wherever any
other bridge or ferry is so near that it injures the franchise, or di-
minishes the toll in a positive and essential degree, there it is a
nuisance, and is actionable. It invades the franchise, and ought to
be abated."

Story had a powerful point. Suppose, he hypothesized, the legislature said to investors: build a bridge, bear the burdens of maintenance, and collect the tolls. Suppose the legislature offered no
guarantee that the corporation could receive its tolls and reserved
the right to erect competing bridges anywhere. "[I]s there a man
living, of ordinary discretion or prudence, who would have accepted
such a charter upon such terms," Story asked. And what legislature, in its right senses, he continued, would have ever inserted
such a qualification and expected a response from private capital
and patronage? When the legislature chartered the Warren Bridge
in 1828, and provided that it ultimately be free, the effect on the
Charles River Bridge tolls was the same as if the legislature had
directly abrogated them.

Significantly, Taney had avoided any direct treatment of this
consideration, but he probably subscribed to the underlying assumptions of the free bridge proponents in the local squabble. The
proprietors had taken a great risk but had been amply rewarded
beyond their expectations. The stock values had risen excessively
on speculations of even greater prospects as the community developed. The proprietors and their immediate heirs had profited
handsomely, and with that consideration, the community was
scarcely obligated to continue paying a tribute to an unproductive,
uncreative *rentier* class. Taney ignored the theoretical implications,

and like the community, undoubtedly preferred to think in terms of practical and current conditions.

Story apparently realized that his common law erudition and scholarship amounted to an exercise in futility. And he was not totally obtuse toward the temper of the times. He realized the impact of technological change and the need for its implementation; he was certainly not adverse to material progress. Though Taney did stand for the "onrushing railroad," it is unfair to stigmatize Story as a "horse and buggy" judge. Taney and Story disagreed on the judicial interpretation of charters and contracts. But it was a difference over the means to the same end. Both favored a public policy that would encourage and foster improvements. Taney emphasized opportunity—immediate opportunity—as the chief inducement for investments, whereas Story recognized security of title and full enjoyment of existing property as paramount.

Story confidently believed that investors must be assured the security and productiveness of their capital; otherwise public improvements based on private capital would come to a halt. He found it paradoxical that a successful venture should threaten the security of investments: "If the government means to invite its citizens to enlarge the public comforts and conveniences, to establish bridges, turnpikes, or canals, or railroads, there must be some pledge, that the property will be safe; that the enjoyment will be coextensive with the grant, and that success will not be the signal of a general combination to overthrow its rights, and to take away its profits." The current agitation against corporate privileges, he warned, would only alarm potential investors against participating in public enterprises. Yet Story knew better. In his own way, he perceived the irony and sham of the Charles River Bridge controversy when he observed that his native Massachusetts, in order to assure improvements, made grants of exclusive privileges to the new railroads.

Story, moreover, recognized the problems raised by obsolete privileges, such as those of turnpike and canal companies. But the just manner of treating such impediments to progress and public improvements, Story believed, lay within the state's power of eminent domain. In this manner the state served the community's purpose and protected the rights of property. He dismissed the defendants' contention that the damage caused by the new bridge was merely consequential and therefore the state was not liable. Once again, Story refused to recognize any distinction between a direct and an indirect method. The "eternal principles of justice," he averred, required compensation.

Story simply discounted the potentially staggering social and economic costs to the community inherent in a universal application of eminent domain—even if those costs restrained and inhibited further development. The difference with Taney is again significant. The Chief Justice ignored the question of eminent domain in part because it was not at issue; the state was not a party in the case. Furthermore, once he determined the proper means of charter construction, Taney could avoid the issue of eminent domain. Carrying the Court with him on the validity of strict construction, Taney disposed of the compensation question and focused on the need for recognizing broadly-shared commonwealth values. His abiding concern was with the will and needs of the larger community; some individuals' rights had to be sacrificed in behalf of ambitious other individuals. Allegedly, this would better serve the needs of the whole community. To the very end, however, Story emphasized the rights of individuals and a potential legislative despotism. The burden was on the state to prevent any misconception of public intentions. If the legislature did not mean to grant exclusive rights, it should say so. The grantees, he added, then act at their own peril, and they "must abide the results of their overweening confidence, indiscretion, and zeal."

Story's tragic sense of moral decay in the midst of commercial greed and untoward ambitions echoed the simple messages of honor and duty. The price of honor for him was no less than the value Taney placed on progress. Perhaps, though, like Taney, Story understood the political and social pressures that had so often dominated the bridge controversy. If so, he undoubtedly considered them beneath contempt. They did violence to the law he revered, a law he believed had amply and usefully fostered growth, progress, and above all, justice.

VIII

THE
LOCAL IMPACT

LAW, AS ROSCOE POUND once wrote, "must be judged by the results it achieves, not by the niceties of its internal structure." There are various ways to observe the impact of important constitutional decisions. There are, first, the local and contemporary ramifications of such cases. The Supreme Court's ruling in the Charles River Bridge affair after all involved a vital question for the state of Massachusetts, the Boston-Charlestown area, and, on a very personal level, the shareholders of the bridge corporation. What change, what resolution, then, did the decision bring to the participants? Also what was the reception of, and the reaction to, the decision by larger forces in the nation—by political groups, by economic interests? This problem is linked with the larger one of attitudes toward the Supreme Court. The Charles River Bridge case, in conjunction with other cases during the same term, aroused a great deal of discussion and controversy about the Supreme Court. For the first time since the Marshall Court's great constitutional decisions in the first two decades of the century, the 1837 decisions raised fundamental questions about constitutional interpretation and the judicial role. Did the various decisions mark important constitutional and institutional change? Was there, as some frightened contemporaries and later historians contended, a judicial revolution in 1837? Or did the anticipated fears of contemporary commentators magnify and distort a slight alteration of judicial behavior? Finally, what was the meaning of the Charles River Bridge case for future litigation, especially that related to technological change, economic growth, and the power of government? In brief, what were its uses, what results did it achieve, and what were its social and economic effects?

#   #   #

As the Charles River Bridge case neared its climax in Washington, there were renewed efforts to resolve the issues in Massachusetts. The basic problem still involved the recognition of the demands for the establishment of free avenues over the Charles on the one hand, and equity—specifically in the form of compensation—for the proprietors of the old bridge. For the free bridge advocates, the demands were mutually exclusive; for the proprietors, however, they were inextricably bound together. Principles and positions had hardened since the chartering of the Warren Bridge in 1828. In reality, there was an irreconcilable tension between the divergent forces. Each was so completely wedded to his respective point of view that any weakening, any sacrifice, would have been tantamount to conceding the validity of the other's principles.

Although the Charles River Bridge proprietors had failed to prevent the construction of the Warren Bridge, the protracted litigation in the state and federal courts delayed the achievement of the ostensible goal of their antagonists—a free bridge over the Charles. There was an understandable concern by public officials to maintain the tolls pending the outcome of the suit in Washington, both to provide funds for maintenance of the bridge and to establish a contingency fund for possible damages assessed against the Warren Bridge Corporation.

The Warren Bridge's earnings far exceeded early estimates. Within two years the tolls paid for the original costs of the bridge. According to the charter, the bridge should have reverted to the state at that point. But the legislature and the corporate officers feared that an adverse decision in the pending case could result in costly damages; accordingly the legislature extended the tolls in March 1832 for another year. With the failure of the Supreme Court to settle the case, the legislature had to wrestle with the matter of tolls again the following year. An act passed in March 1833 provided, as one alternative, that the bridge be turned over to the state, with the governor assuming the defense in the suit. The tolls were to continue; state agents would collect them and place the funds in the general treasury. But another proviso allowed the Warren Bridge proprietors to maintain control if they posted security that they would collect the tolls, maintain the bridge, and turn over all profits to the state. Since they posted bond the state continued to play only an indirect and shadowy role in the legal proceedings.

After the state extended the tolls for a third time in 1834, strong opposition developed to any further continuance. In the spring of 1835, over sixty groups submitted petitions to the legislature demanding complete abolition of the tolls. Popular pressures delayed legislative renewal of the tolls until November 1835. Apparently either the Warren Bridge proprietors or the state desired to end the responsibilities of the corporation. The 1835 act called upon the cities of Boston and Charlestown to give bond that they would perform all the duties of the proprietors by assuming the management of the bridge, and indemnify the Charles River Bridge proprietors if necessary. The state was unwilling, so it appeared, to absorb the burdens and potential costs of the Warren Bridge; rather, the communities most directly involved and affected had to assume the risks as well as the benefits. Charlestown, where interest in the Warren Bridge was greatest, agreed to perform the duties of the corporation, but Boston declined.

Boston's refusal to post bond and share in the management of the new bridge once again raised the problems of the tolls and the state's interest in the Warren Bridge. Perhaps sensing the possibility of a compromise settlement, the Charles River Bridge stockholders submitted a memorial to the legislature on January 20, 1836. Time had not shaken the proprietors' faith in the justice of their position. They maintained that the arguments of the Warren Bridge petitioners during the 1820s—namely, that the 1792 charter extension had been gained by fraud and deception, and that the proprietors' profits had been exorbitant—had no basis in fact. But now in 1836, with the new bridge in place, the proprietors appealed for recompense upon grounds much broader than their own individual interests.

Massachusetts still lacked a clear policy for supporting internal improvements, particularly for railroad development. New York and Pennsylvania, among others, already had financed railroad projects exclusively, or largely, by the states themselves. But the advocates of state aid made little headway in the Bay State during the 1830s, and Massachusetts remained dependent on private capital and initiative. The state simply granted corporate charters with the right to take toll. But in their 1836 memorial, the Charles River Bridge proprietors warned that the state's policy, with its comparatively cheap cost to the citizenry, was endangered if the legislature persisted in its action of 1828 and denied any compensation to the old bridge shareholders. In short, if the legislature set an example of chartering new bridges, canals, or railroads, and thus destroying the value of existing enterprises, private capital would seek other opportunities and the state would have to assume the full burden of internal improvements.

Notwithstanding their concern for the state's future well-being, the proprietors did not entirely neglect their own interest. To guarantee the continued integrity and good faith of the state, along with the still powerful demands for free access into Boston, the proprietors offered another compromise. In exchange for a promise to drop the suit before the Supreme Court, they asked the state to turn over to them all proceeds from the Warren Bridge then in the treasury (over $40,000), and grant them also the net tolls from both bridges for two years. For 1833 and 1834, the net tolls had amounted to $47,649.56. If the legislature preferred to take immediate possession of both bridges, then the proprietors suggested a flat payment of $600 per share to the Charles River Bridge stockholders (or $90,000 for all 150 shares).

The proprietors certainly believed that local conditions might move the legislature to compromise, but they also had their own practical reasons for making this proposal. In January 1835, Webster urged from Washington that they settle the controversy and end the suit. Taney's pending appointment as Associate Justice reinforced Webster's fading hopes for a favorable judgment. "I would be delighted," he wrote, "at any prospect of terminating this law suit by compromise."

Charlestown residents, led once again by John Skinner, wasted little time in submitting a remonstrance to the legislature against the proprietors' memorial. The reply traversed familiar ground, rejecting out of hand the consistent assertions of vested rights. The Charlestown residents contended that the present share-holders had no claim of right against the state; their expectations of profit rested on "the mistaken notion that the corporation was above the law," and that the state could not authorize another bridge during the life of the charter. To settle the controversy, Skinner and his associates called upon the proprietors to drop their suit, "cease all further vexation of the agents of the state who erected the Warren Bridge," and allow the legislature, after a fair and impartial hearing, to ascertain the merits of their claim and provide for a just settlement.

Apparently the Charlestown group, along with others, was prepared ultimately to concede some cash settlement to the Charles River Bridge proprietors by the state. But their immediate concern still centered on the question of tolls. They contended that the Warren Bridge toll had been levied only to reimburse the expenses of construction, a purpose long since achieved. The interest on the tolls collected since 1832 would, they continued, be ample to keep the bridge in repair forever; furthermore, the city of Charlestown was prepared to guarantee maintenance in consideration of the monies collected from tolls since 1832. Finally, the Charlestown residents reminded the legislature that the Warren Bridge had been built because public exigencies required another avenue, and one ultimately meant to be free; they consequently concluded that "any toll beyond what is necessary for the repairs of the bridge would be an abuse of power."

Following receipt of the Charles River Bridge proprietors' memorial, the legislature appointed a joint select committee to examine the claims and formulate legislative action. The committee had several alternatives. It could follow the recommendations of the Charlestown group and declare the Warren Bridge toll free; or it could devise a compensation scheme acceptable to the Charles River Bridge proprietors; or it could maintain the status quo. The latter involved an extension of tolls on the new bridge for another year as action by the Supreme Court seemed unlikely at the moment.

Despite the deadlock in the Supreme Court and the impending personnel changes, the joint committee still feared an adverse decision. Therefore they rejected any resolution which did not include provision for terminating the case. As long as the proprietors remained free to pursue their suit, the committee recognized the possibility of "disastrous" consequences "to the interests of the state and the public." Compromise, with some compensation, dominated the committee's deliberations. The committee members wanted to end the controversy, protect the Warren Bridge corporation from damages, and insure that the public not be deprived of an accommodation that could be permanently secured by a comparatively moderate expense. To these ends, they recommended immediate free access across both bridges, and suggested that compensation to the Charles River Bridge proprietors be "promptly and efficiently provided." Significantly, the committee never conceded the proprietors' legal rights to compensation; rather, it was, as the committee insisted, "a matter of expediency."

The joint committee seemed genuinely anxious to preserve both bridges across the Charles. Either demographic and economic realities now required two avenues, or the legislators truly believed their own arguments of the previous decade. The committee members argued that if they could not do something in behalf of the old bridge proprietors, the bridge would fall into decay, become unfit for use, and then the legislature would be pressed by claims for another bridge: "The same public necessity and convenience which required the construction of Warren bridge, . . . will call for the construction of a new one to supply the place of the Charles River bridge. . . . Interest, then, as well as the settlement of a protracted controversy, urge upon the legislature the adoption of such measures as shall secure the surrender . . . of the franchise."

While making no specific recommendation for the amount of compensation, the committee suggested that the toll on the Warren Bridge be extended until March 1837, when the pool would be approximately $45,000. Apparently, this was the anticipated settlement amount, for the committee's report suggested that compensation come from tolls collected on the Warren Bridge. But the committee soon sensed that the $45,000 figure would not command widespread support, for a bill introduced by one of its members in the Senate on February 18 set compensation at $25,000. The settlement was contingent upon the proprietors surrendering their franchise and dropping their suit by May 1, 1836. Tolls were to continue on both bridges, but if either Boston or Charlestown posted bond—this time the legislature would accept the security of either town—the guarantors would receive the tolls in the treasury and both avenues would become free. Finally, in the event that the Charles River Bridge proprietors did not convey their franchise, either city could still assume the escrowed tolls and the responsibility for maintenance, and the Warren Bridge would be free.

A week later the old bridge proprietors submitted another memorial, rejecting the offer of $25,000. Their legislative friends then attempted to amend the bill and raise the compensation figure to $40,000, but the Senate defeated the measure, 15-19. The Charles River Bridge supporters then sought another extension of the Warren Bridge toll collections. After failing to gain an increased compensation, the strategy was apparently to preserve the status quo and continue tolls for both bridges, thereby building a larger fund for a possible award of damages. The free bridge advocates, however, immediately sensed the ploy. In the House, Representative Robert Rantoul of Charlestown flatly charged that the proposal gave "time for further maneuvres" to the Charles River Bridge proprietors. Rantoul and others were out of patience with further delays. "Ought the House," Rantoul asked, "be perpetually stung by the same serpent?" Representative Thomas Whittemore expressed similar sentiments and warned the House that the popular clamor for a free bridge could no longer be denied. He did not know, Whittemore said, "what would be the consequence, if the long and weary expectation of the people should be further dallied with." The bill merely extending the Warren Bridge tolls came to a Senate vote on March 1, and lost, 12-18.

With the original proposal containing provision for a $25,000 compensation unacceptable to the Charles River Bridge proprietors, and with the failure to continue the tolls for another year, the Warren Bridge became the property of the state and—at long last—a free avenue. The city of Charlestown celebrated with a cannon salute and festivities in the town hall. Legislators and state officials came free of charge; citizens of "the community" paid one dollar.

The victory of the free bridge advocates resolved a longstanding conflict within the state concerning the wisdom and validity of levying tolls on publicly owned improvements. A wide-ranging debate preceded the bridge's reversion to the state. Basically, the battle was between those who favored operation of the bridges free from toll, except for the amount necessary for maintenance, and those who advocated retention of the tolls in order to accumulate funds for improvements in other parts of the state. At issue here were divergent views of the scope and commonalty of community interest as the determinant of social cost accounting.

Those who favored "free" bridges considered only those who used the avenues as constituting a community. Tolls excessive of maintenance costs, they argued, were not only unreasonable and oppressive, but unfair particularly because they amounted to an improportionate tax. Those who maintained that the state should continue tolls took a broader conception of community interest. They conceded the desirability of good, free roads and bridges, and their necessity for the prosperity of the commonwealth. But they insisted that the whole state should share in this advantage; accordingly, as long as some areas remained deprived of any roads or bridges, tolls should be collected in order to finance further projects in the underdeveloped areas. In other words, they based their accounting formula on the idea that the whole expense of internal improvements, for the entire state, constituted one integral charge, and that the costs might be defrayed by charging those portions of the community that had obtained their projects so that others might secure theirs in the future.

In 1835, the legislature sought counsel from the state attorney general on the legal points at stake in this controversy. But in his report, the attorney general largely eschewed legal doctrine and correctly assessed the issue as one of public policy and largely dependent upon political pressures and choices. As if anticipating the considerations which forced the freeing of Warren Bridge a year later, the attorney general questioned the willingness of people to accept continued assessments after the original costs had been defrayed. The answer came in 1836 when the legislature bowed to the demands of the smaller community for a free bridge. In this case, Charlestown's "community of interest" with the rest of the state extended no further than making common cause for the destruction of the old toll bridge.

With the Warren Bridge a free avenue, the Charles River Bridge proprietors now awaited the outcome of the case in Washington. Travel over their bridge, according to most reports, virtually ceased; the individual shares were worthless unless there were some settlement. But once more, following a meeting of the corporation on April 2, the proprietors submitted a public protest to the legislature. It reflected no tone of conciliation or hint of compromise; instead, it revealed only great bitterness with the final triumph of their Charlestown adversaries. But the proprietors reserved their greatest invective for the legislature, which step by step, culminating in the decision to make the Warren Bridge free, had "completely annihilated the property in Charles river bridge." And, it was duly noted, charitable and literary institutions, or widows and orphans, owned one-third of that property. The proprietors vowed to press their legal claims and "never to submit to . . . acts of clear and manifest injustice." Perhaps sensing the futility of further appeals to the legislature, the proprietors sounded a final warning for other investors and for the future of public enterprises:

> Are charters inviolable, or are they not? Are they repealable at the will of the Legislature, or are they not? Is property invested upon the faith of them confiscable at the pleasure of the government, or is it not? Can private property be taken for public uses, real or pretended, without making compensation to the owners? Can the public good, in the judgment of honest and enlightened men, ever require, in any case, such manifest violation of private right, and such sacrifice of individual property? Or, if an enlightened Legislature could possibly be supposed to disregard the dictates of justice, can the great cause of public improvement through the means of individual enterprise, be expected to be carried forward, while such examples as that which has been furnished in the case of the Charles river bridge are before the eyes of men?

The Supreme Court's final disposition of the Charles River Bridge case in February 1837 ended once and for all any claims for damages the proprietors might lay against the state. They then cast aside the defiance and bitterness of a year earlier and submitted completely to the mercy and charity of the legislature. The terms of their charter still obligated them to perform certain functions, such as keeping the bridge in repair, lighting it, tending the draw for the passage of vessels, and paying Harvard College its annual annuity of $666. The proprietors had fulfilled their obligations for the past year while competing with the free bridge, during a time when their income did not come close to meeting expenses. Accordingly, they petitioned the legislature for relief in March 1837, asking specifically to be released from their

obligations. In addition, they requested a "reasonable compensation" for the loss of their property, thereby allowing the community
another free bridge. The *Independent Chronicle and Boston Patriot,*
a Whig organ that had backed the proprietors' cause, accepted the
rationale of consequential damages, but maintained that the
similar forms of property in this case justified some payment of
compensation. The newspaper appeared willing to abide by the
judicial result however misguided it was, but it urged the state
now to come forward, preserve its honor, and compensate the
proprietors.

The legislature's reply was somewhat petulant. A joint committee acknowledged the proprietors' burdens and admitted that
unless the state took some action, the bridge would have to close.
But it designed proposals only to delay any final settlement. The
joint committee presented resolutions establishing another in-
vestigating committee, specifically authorized to determine the
value of the bridge, the value of the corporation, including its
right to take tolls, and whether any of the communities affected
would contribute to the support of maintaining two free bridges.
In addition, the joint committee recommended that the state take
immediate possession of the Charles River Bridge, continue the
existing tolls, and support its maintenance with funds reserved
for repair of the Warren Bridge. The proprietors meanwhile
would reserve their legal rights under the charter and could
resume control a year later if there were no satisfactory settlement. In short, the state would not pay immediate compensation,
but it would assume the bridge's liabilities for a minimum of one
year. The full legislature accepted the resolves, but in one last fit
of vindictiveness—or perhaps assertion of principle—struck out
the section providing for a determination of the value of the
franchise.

The proprietors, too, had a final gesture of defiance. On May 3,
1837 they raised the draw, and closed their bridge to further
traffic. Following the proprietors' action, the legislature apparently
lost interest in the matter, and the joint committee never delivered
its promised report. In his annual messages in 1838 and 1839,

Governor Edward Everett urged the legislators to settle the matter on "liberal and equitable principles." The communities, he said, must have use of both bridges and there must be some sort of compensation; "public convenience and private right," declared Everett, "seem to call loudly for some definitive arrangements." Petitions to the legislature urged that the Charles River Bridge be re-opened, but the impasse continued.

The election of Jacksonian Democrat Marcus Morton in late 1839 dashed the proprietors' slender hopes for a prompt settlement. Morton, it will be recalled, had delivered the leading opinion in the state supreme court's decision almost a decade earlier; he had denied every premise of the proprietors and had anticipated Taney's final disposition of the case. His legislative message of January 1840 made no direct reference to the bridge controversy. He pledged that the state would honor "every valid engagement . . . made in its behalf," but the tone of his remarks indicated a willingness only to fulfill bona fide contractual arrangements. Furthermore, his call for financial retrenchment indicated little sympathy with "liberal" settlements based on the generosity of the state. Finally, Morton's views on public policy toward internal improvements also seemed to preclude any grant of compensation. The state, the governor insisted, must avoid expenditures that did not accrue "general and equal benefits" for the whole of the population.

The election of the Whig, John Davis, as governor the following year, sparked the fortunes of the Charles River Bridge proprietors. Davis, too, had been a prominent adversary, serving with Simon Greenleaf as counsel for the Warren Bridge in the final arguments before the Supreme Court in Washington. At that time, Davis repeatedly had argued that the proprietors were not entitled to damages as of right; whatever losses they had suffered were only consequential and neither the state nor the Warren Bridge corporation were liable. But with Greenleaf, Davis had hinted that the state, with a "just regard for its honor," could be trusted to provide some compensation.

The election of Davis as governor, combined with some changes in the political cast of the legislature, worked to produce an act in March 1841 that offered a $25,000 settlement to the proprietors in exchange for the surrender of their charter. To cover the cost of the settlement and to repair the now badly dilapidated bridge, the legislature reinstituted the tolls at the old rate on both bridges in order to raise the compensation amount and a $50,000 maintenance fund. The collection of tolls was not to exceed two years. The Charles River Bridge proprietors accepted the legislature's offer a week after passage. Five years earlier, the proprietors had rejected a similar offer, gambling, in effect, on a favorable Supreme Court verdict. Now, in 1841, there was nothing to do but succumb to the legislature's judgment of equity and generosity. For the widows and orphans, and whoever else held Charles River Bridge stock, the legislature's settlement amounted to $166.66 per share.

There was one other account to settle—the Harvard College annuity. When the Warren Bridge became a free avenue in 1836 the annual payments of $666.66 to the College ceased. A few weeks later, the Charles River Bridge proprietors notified the College that they no longer could make any payments. But finally in 1847 the legislature voted a grant of $3,333.30 to the College as compensation for the loss of its annuity during the years in which the state possessed the bridge. Still, the College suffered substantial losses. In 1814 it had purchased two shares of stock at a cost of $4,160; following the 1847 settlement, the College's losses, with interest, thus came to over ninety per cent. With the annuity payment of 1847, the College had some hope that it would continue in the future. Not so. This was the last recognition of Harvard's "ancient" ferry rights.

#   #   #

The political settlement of the Charles River Bridge affair marked a total victory for the state and the principles it advocated. The old bridge proprietors had been decisively routed. Their compensation of $25,000 was a mere pittance in view of the stakes involved; it hardly qualified even as conscience money.

That figure was less than the combined tolls for the two bridges in 1834, and considering the rapid growth in population and commerce for the area, the probable tolls for the remaining fifteen years of the Charles River Bridge charter made even the proprietors' 1836 request for $90,000 modest indeed. The 1841 settlement really conceded nothing to the proprietors' legal and public policy positions. The $25,000 did not represent payment for past damages; instead it merely constituted the state's purchase of the proprietors' rights to maintain a bridge for the remaining years of their charter. Seen in that light, the proprietors had no choice. Their bridge had no future value as a revenue-producing investment so long as it had to compete with the free Warren Bridge.

Nor was the state's settlement any concession to its adversaries' position on public policy, specifically as it related to future investments. The defenders of the Charles River Bridge had consistently maintained that the state's capricious and indiscriminate destruction of the proprietors' "property"—that is, their tolls—would frighten and discourage potential investors in public projects. Legal and constitutional requirements notwithstanding, this argument probably had the greatest logic and appeal throughout the state. The legislature, however, remained unimpressed. There was no perceptible, alarming decline in public investments. Furthermore, the legislators knew that public sentiment did not support any generous compensation for an "odious monopoly." It was difficult for the legislature, let alone the public, to distinguish the fabulous returns earned by the original and early investors from those who had purchased stock in the Charles River Bridge only just prior to 1828. In his state supreme court opinion in 1830, Chief Justice Parker had observed that the question of indemnifying the proprietors had been prejudiced because of the enormous profits returned through the years. According to Parker, if the legislature had chartered a competing bridge shortly after the first was completed, when "its success could be only conjectural, and the experiment of its durability was scarcely tried," condemnation of the legislature would have been "universal." But the bridge's forty years of financial success obscured public memories of the initial risks, and by the 1830s, the shareholders were vulnerable against the legislative and judicial literal construction of their rights.

The nature of the settlement in 1841 offered one other revelation of the legislature's view of social cost accounting. The $25,000 payment to the Charles River Bridge proprietors was not a charge against the whole state. Instead, tolls on both bridges redeemed the state bonds which funded the $25,000. So those most immediately affected, the bridges' users, paid one more bit of ransom for their precious free bridges.

IX

THE "REVOLUTION" OF 1837

THE NATIONAL REACTION to the Charles River Bridge case occurred in response to that particular decision, to other important constitutional rulings during the same Supreme Court term, and to the nature of the institution itself. The Taney Court decisions of 1837 alternately pleased and shocked important political and economic segments of American society. Although reactions differed, there was a widespread perception that these decisions were part of a judicial revolution, with far-reaching consequences for change.

Public critics of the Charles River Bridge decision took their cue from Daniel Webster, who contended that the Court had overturned the contract clause and had thereby endangered private property. Critics charged that the decision was part of a triumphant "agrarian radicalism" that subverted "the principles of law and property." A Whig correspondent reported to his Boston newspaper that property held under charter privileges was no longer secure, and advised investors to find other outlets for their capital.

Chancellor James Kent offered an elaborate public attack in the pages of the *New York Review*. Generally following, and ap-

proving, Story's dissent, Kent berated the Court for abandoning
the "well-understood and solid" common law principles of charter
construction. He reviewed the history and setting of the original
Charles River Bridge charter, and contended that the proprietors'
risks, burdens, and duties, all of which were directed toward
useful and beneficial purposes for the community, entitled them
to a liberal interpretation of their charter rights. The state's
decision to charter a new bridge was, in Kent's mind, immoral
and illegal. He regarded it as settled in common law that all
grants of franchise contained an implication that everything
necessary to holding and enjoying the franchise was likewise
granted.

Democrats who praised the Charles River Bridge decision, and
condemned the Court's critics, spoke in the most commonplace
Jacksonian rhetoric. The *Detroit Free Press,* for example, lauded the
decision for establishing "the great republican principle that a
grant is not a monopoly or a vested right." In more simple terms,
Democratic partisans praised the decision for its "overthrow"
of the "whole Whig doctrine of vested rights." Enthusiastic Democratic free bridge spokesmen in the Boston area hailed the
decision as "a glorious triumph of free principles over monopoly;
of enlightened liberality over bigoted exclusiveness; of the rights
of the many over the usurpations of the few." The Court's "glorious blow," commented a Boston editor, had destroyed "the
aristocratic props that have enabled the privileged few to prey
upon the burdened many." The same Boston editor did not miss
the partisan significance of the decision. The victory against
monopoly, he said, had been won by Democratic judges with
Democratic principles. He berated Story's Whiggish views and
the "bigoted blockheads" whose common law writings Story had
so slavishly followed.

Democrats took special satisfaction from the Whig criticism that
politics inspired the Supreme Court's decision. For this constituted
a recognition of longstanding Democratic contentions that the
Court was a political institution serving distinct political, social,
and economic interests. A Whig writer bitterly complained of

"the spectacle of a tribunal completely revolutionized by a party, and composed of party leaders." One Democratic commentator, replying to Chancellor Kent, noted the sudden shift in the judge's attitude toward the Court, a Court he once regarded as "the palladium" of American liberties. But now, as the writer noted, "with his political friends no longer in the ascendant," Kent regarded the Court's doctrines as "desolating."

Reflecting their newly-gained confidence in the federal judiciary, the Democrats at last passed a new judiciary act in March 1837. Since 1802, when Jefferson and his congressional supporters had repealed the Federalist-sponsored Judiciary Act of 1801, Democratic congressmen had resisted expanding the federal judiciary despite pressing national needs. Numerous states in the south and west, which had joined the Union since the turn of the century, were unrepresented in any judicial circuit. Every president after Jefferson had recommended an increase in the inferior courts, but partisan and institutional rivalries in Congress prevented reform. Finally, on March 3, 1837—Jackson's last day in office—the Democratic-controlled Congress passed a bill adding two new judicial circuits and increasing the size of the Supreme Court from seven to nine members.* In one of his last actions, Jackson nominated two new justices and apparently secured Democratic domination of the high court.

#   #   #

The contemporary notion of a judicial revolution in 1837 stemmed from the belief that the Taney Court decisions had over-turned the settled doctrines of the Marshall Court. Justice Joseph Story abetted this idea by his outraged dissents against the new dispensation and his impassioned defense of older standards. Significantly, the 1837 cases had carried over from Marshall's tenure but had not been resolved for various reasons. The relevant cases in addition to the Charles River Bridge case were *New York v. Miln,* in which the Court clarified the federal commerce power,

*Prior to Reconstruction, Supreme Court members represented and regularly served each of the judicial circuits.

and *Briscoe* v. *Bank of Kentucky,* which reflected a more permissive attitude toward state bank note issues. The Charles River Bridge case seemed a repudiation of *Dartmouth College* v. *Woodward,* the *Miln* decision as a refutation of Marshall's nationalistic goals in *Gibbons* v. *Ogden,* and *Briscoe* as a direct reversal of Marshall's denial of state power to emit bills of credit in *Craig* v. *Missouri.* Story dissented from all three rulings in 1837, regularly invoking the "old law" and the opinions of the late Chief Justice, whose name, Story said, ought "never to be pronounced without reverence." The justice's public statements left no doubt that the decisions reflected a wholesale change in judicial attitudes; to Mrs. Story he was even more explicit: "The old constitutional doctrines are fading fast away, and a change has come over the public mind, from which I augur little good."

Chancellor Kent was Story's kindred spirit on legal and constitutional issues. The 1837 decisions, and particularly the Charles River Bridge decision, shocked the old New York Federalist. Deeply distressed by Jacksonian Democracy as it operated in Washington and in his native state, Kent believed that the Supreme Court would resist the revolutionary ardor of the times and preserve the nation's legal and constitutional heritage. The Charles River Bridge decision shocked him, and a re-reading of the opinions left him with "increased disgust." His last hope was shattered. Despondently, he told Story that he had lost "confidence and hope in the constitutional guardianship and protection of the Supreme Court."

To Kent, in turn, Story revealed his deepest feelings regarding the "evil of the change" and "sad times" that had come over the Court since the loss of Chief Justice Marshall—"our great support, and our truest glory," as the Justice piously characterized him. Although he had decided to remain on the bench, Story realized the futility of his position. There were, he told Kent, "no hopes for the future, and with the deepest sense, that all, which for twenty-five years I have aided in building up, in the doctrines of constitutional law, are to be directly or indirectly overturned; slowly, if not suddenly; by fragments, if not in masses." But more than the changes of specific doctrines, Story deplored what he perceived as a change in judicial philosophy and perception of role within the Supreme Court. Great judges, he said, must have "a supreme reverence for the Law and a firmness to maintain its principles against the temper of the Times, and the fluctuating policy of party spirit." But now, surrounded by the despised Jackson's appointees, Story lamented the triumph of what he called the Jeffersonian dogma "that the Judges should represent and be made to feel the force of public and popular opinion." And thus Story characterized himself as "the last Relic of the old school — in the midst of the Desolation."

Many Jacksonian Democrats agreed with Story's analysis, if not his mood. They concurred in his conclusion that there was a profound change not only in the Court's personnel, but in its doctrines as well. With Taney's appointment in March 1836, Democratic publicists such as William Leggett had predicted that the new Chief Justice, with the other Jacksonian jurists, would produce a doctrinal revolution. After the 1837 decisions, there were cautious judgments that such a change had indeed occurred.

The 1837 decisions that aroused such despair and exultation involved cardinal points of contention in American constitutional history — namely, state attitudes toward public contracts, the regulation of commerce, and the problem of paper currency. These issues were also conditioned by the more emotional one concerning the division of national and state powers. The Confederation era witnessed repeated conflicts over these matters and the Constitution was framed, to some extent, specifically to resolve them. Yet the new national powers remained somewhat ambiguous. Coupled with local pressures and needs, and the absence of effective national policy, state legislatures continued to act in these areas. Inevitably, their most controversial actions resulted in litigation and action by the Supreme Court.

The lack of national power to regulate commerce among the several states was one of the more obvious weaknesses in the Articles of Confederation. Trade wars and tariffs on goods exchanged between the states inhibited commercial growth and the development of a large common national market in which goods could flow unencumbered by artificial restraints. The new constitution specifically authorized Congress to regulate interstate, as well as foreign, commerce. But exactly what constituted commerce? And did this mean all commerce? Did the states retain concurrent jurisdiction? Could the states regulate interstate commerce in the absence of federal regulations? Could the federal government regulate commercial activities that occurred wholly within one state?

Although the desire to secure national power over interstate commerce figured prominently in the drive for a new constitution, surprisingly little controversy concerning the scope and meaning of that power developed during the first decades of the new republic. The Supreme Court's first opportunity to deal with the commerce power at length did not come until *Gibbons* v. *Ogden* in 1824. That case involved a conflict between New York laws granting exclusive steamboat privileges upon the navigable waters of the state and preexisting federal statutes providing for the licensing of ships engaged in the coastal trade.

John Marshall's *Gibbons* opinion was one of his last great efforts to impose a highly nationalistic construction upon the Constitution, interpreting it, as he said, with "safe and fundamental principles to sustain the authority of the national government." First, Marshall offered a broad definition of the term "commerce," contending that it meant more than merely the exchange of commodities. Commerce, the Chief Justice said, "is undoubtedly traffic, but it is more; it is intercourse" and, as such, comprehended control of navigable waters. Furthermore, congressional authority did not end at the external boundaries of states, but could follow commerce "introduced into the interior." Marshall also maintained that Congress's power to regulate such commerce "is complete in itself, may be exercised to its utmost extent, and acknowledges no limitations, other than are prescribed in the Constitution." Despite such sweeping statements, Marshall hedged his position regarding the knotty problem of concurrent state power. Whatever his personal views, the Chief Justice disavowed Daniel Webster's

(Webster appeared as counsel for Gibbons) extreme nationalistic argument that the mere existence of congressional power precluded state action in all cases. Instead, Marshall acknowledged that states retained control over matters relating solely to internal commerce within their boundaries, and that unless the two directly conflicted, state regulations of commerce could exist concurrently with those of the federal government.

But three years later, in *Brown* v. *Maryland,* Marshall attempted to expand the potential of national power, even in matters where Congress had not acted. In this case, the Court voided a Maryland statute requiring a license for importers of out-of-state goods, ruling that as long as the goods remained in the "original package," the states could not impose a tax. Most importantly, the *Brown* decision established the idea that some state actions positively discriminating against interstate commerce were unconstitutional despite congressional inaction. Nevertheless, in *Willson* v. *Blackbird Creek Marsh Company* (1829), the Court adhered to practical tests and rejected the notion of exclusive national power. The state of Delaware had authorized the building of a dam across a navigable stream. A federally-licensed ship broke down the dam and subsequently was brought to court in a trespass action. The owners of the sloop argued in their defense that the dam had interfered with the right to use the navigable waters of the United States, subject only to congressional regulations and restrictions. The plaintiffs, however, contended that the state had authority over the creek, which ran exclusively within its boundaries. In the absence of any federal statute regarding the navigable waters of Delaware, Chief Justice Marshall sustained the state's right to build the dam. Significantly, his opinion was a fillip for the exercise of state police powers. He accepted the state's argument that damming the creek enhanced property values and improved the health of the inhabitants by keeping water out of the marshes. According to Marshall, so long as Congress had not acted upon the subject, the state was free to act.

The Marshall Court's commerce clause doctrines were ambiguous at best. Despite broad hints of national supremacy, there were significant qualifications. Congressional authority, it was clear, did not preempt the field. States could act separately in the absence of federal legislation and as long as the laws were not in conflict could apparently exercise concurrent jurisdiction. But though Marshall had conceded some latitude to state police authority, he never suggested that it could be superior to Congress's commerce power.

In *New York* v. *Miln,* however, the Taney Court seemed to take a step in that direction. The case involved a New York law requiring ship captains to report the vital statistics of every passenger they landed at the port of New York. Miln, a ship captain, failed to report the information and was fined for noncompliance. Miln's attorneys argued in his defense that the state law constituted a regulation of commerce that was exclusively the province of Congress. But counsel for the city of New York maintained that in the absence of conflicting federal legislation the state had acted within its rights. Significantly, the New York lawyers disavowed any notions of state sovereignty, but insisted that state laws must stand until Congress acted. The New York law was, they said, a proper police regulation that did not derive from any authority to regulate commerce, but was inherent in any government's power to protect the people of its domain.

Although the Court fragmented in its reasoning, all the justices, with the exception of Story, sustained the New York law. The essential and practical implication of the decision was that such state action was valid in the absence of conflicting federal laws. In that sense, there was little deviation from John Marshall's position; indeed, the Court's acceptance of the local benefits of the police power paralleled Marshall's reasoning in the Delaware dam case. But Justice Philip Barbour's opinion, which was recorded as the majority view,* placed an exaggerated emphasis upon the police power, seemingly at the expense of federal supremacy. Barbour, appointed to the Court with Taney in 1836, was a

---

*In the *Passenger Cases* twelve years later, it was revealed that Barbour did not speak for a majority of the Court in 1837. But a majority agreed that the New York law was constitutional. (7 Howard 283, 429, 431-432)

Virginia Democrat, with well-known state supremacy leanings.

Barbour refused to view the New York law as a regulation of commerce; instead, he viewed it as a police measure designed to protect the community from criminals and paupers. Following this tack, he completely skirted any discussion of the meaning and extent of the federal commerce power. As there was no conflicting federal law, Barbour found Marshall's Gibbons opinion simply inapplicable and instead exalted the police power. For him, it was not only the state's right, but its "bounden and solemn duty," to "advance the safety, happiness and prosperity" of its constituents, "and to provide for [their] . . . general welfare, by any and every act of legislation, which it may deem to be conducive to these ends," so long as the particular power was not restrained by the federal constitution. In matters affecting internal police, Barbour maintained that the state's authority was complete, unqualified, and exclusive. Here Barbour added a new dimension to the ambiguity of the commerce power; his conception of commerce was vague at best, and it was altogether unclear as to when, if at all, federal power could supersede state policy authority.*

Story alertly recognized the potentialities for state powers and the corollary of national impotence in Barbour's opinion. Dissenting, and with the "consolation" that Marshall had agreed with him, Story followed the holding in Gibbons v. Ogden that the carrying of passengers constituted commerce. Thus the New York statute was a regulation of commerce, and the police power was not at issue. Perhaps appalled at Barbour's emphasis, Story moved to the other extreme and contended that federal commerce power

---

*The Miln case, along with subsequent commerce power controversies before the Taney Court, was decided against the backdrop of southern (and sometimes northern) concerns regarding slavery and the migration of free Negroes. There was some fear among the justices that unrestrained federal commerce power might hamper the interstate slave trade or preclude a state's right to exclude undesirable elements. Even when the Court struck down state regulations of commerce, as in the Passenger Cases, some of the majority justices conceded that a state could bar Negroes from its territory. Justice Grier, a Pennsylvanian, described this right in terms of a "sacred law of self-defence, which no power granted to Congress can restrain or annul." (7 Howard 283, 456 [1849])

was exclusive and the states could not interfere, the police power notwithstanding.

Briscoe v. *Bank of Kentucky,* the third important constitutional law decision of the term, involved the highly-charged issue of state-issued paper money. Like both the Charles River Bridge and the *Miln* cases, *Briscoe* had first been argued before the Marshall Court. Article I, Section 10 of the Constitution specifically prohibited the states from issuing bills of credit. The chaos and conflicts over paper money following the Revolution had contributed significantly to dissatisfaction and concern with the Articles of Confederation. Like the regulation of commerce, the control of exchange seemed to dictate a uniform national policy. But as with the commerce clause, there was a wide spectrum of opinion as to the Constitution's meaning.

In 1830, in *Craig* v. *Missouri,* John Marshall again applied his intimate experience and knowledge of the Confederation and the formation of the Constitution in order to subjugate independent state policies. The case involved Missouri loan certificates that were negotiable and used as a medium of exchange within the state. Defining bills of credit in the light of the Confederation experience, Marshall believed that they denoted any paper medium used for exchange purposes. Although Missouri had not stipulated that the loan certificates were legal tender, they fell within the scope of Marshall's wide-ranging definition of bills of credit and hence were unconstitutional. There was significant dissent within the Court, centering chiefly on Marshall's construction of the constitutional prohibition.

The Kentucky bank case in 1837 also involved a state law designed to deal with the acute shortage of currency, a condition common in many of the western states following the War of 1812. In 1820 Kentucky had chartered a bank in which it had sole ownership and control. It authorized the bank to perform the usual banking functions and also to issue notes. Briscoe subsequently challenged the validity of the notes since they constituted state-issued bills of credit. In defense, the state contended that there was a difference between notes issued in the name of the state and those

emitted by a chartered corporation. Furthermore, if state participation through a state-owned corporation made the notes invalid,
then every state bank note was subject to question because all banks
had a state charter.

Speaking for the Court, Justice McLean sustained the state's
arguments and in so doing narrowed Marshall's earlier definition
of bills of credit. McLean limited the meaning of bills of credit to
"paper issued by the sovereign power, containing a pledge of
its faith, and designed to circulate as money." Applied strictly,
McLean's interpretation distinguished between notes issued by the
state in its sovereign capacity from those authorized by its satellite
corporations. McLean accepted the state's assumption that if the
notes of its bank were illegal, then the notes of all state-chartered
banks were similarly invalid since the state could not do indirectly
what it was forbidden to do directly. This rationale and financial
realism dictated constitutional law. For if the Court declared all
state bank notes invalid, then nearly $400 million—"almost the
entire circulating medium of the country," as McLean observed—
would be worthless.

Story's dissent was again a lament for times past. He considered
Marshall's 1830 definition of bills of credit as controlling for the
Kentucky law. Kentucky had, Story believed, merely evaded the
direct prohibition by using an artificial agent. He was contemp-
tuous of McLean's failure to distinguish the state-owned bank's
notes from those of privately-owned, albeit state-chartered, banks.
Finally, he bitterly assailed the majority's expediency, which had
cast the Court and the Constitution "adrift from [their] . . . former
moorings."

Reaction to the 1837 decisions was to some extent framed in
partisan terms. Prominent Whig politicians and newspapers condemned the decisions and were profoundly shaken by the realization of their most pessimistic predictions for the new Jacksonian
court. Some of their Democratic counterparts were similarly unrestrained in approving the decisions and applauding the work of
the new justices. Yet there were Whigs and Democrats alike who
avoided any uncritical partisan rejection or acceptance of the de-

cisions and instead evaluated them in terms of contemporary needs and realities. Thus some Whigs found the decisions not only beneficial, but even reflective of their own ideology; and some Democrats regarded the decisions not as a revolution, or even as a reaction against the extreme nationalism of the Marshall era, but rather as a consolidation of previous doctrines, with the adjustments required by existing realities.

C. S. Davies, a Whig who wrote a lengthy critique of the Court's term in the *North American Review,* regretted the Court's new political orientation, yet admitted that in the long run there was not much difference between the views of Marshall and Taney. Davies deplored the substantive results of the decisions, particularly the paper money issue in *Briscoe,* but in an aside to alarmists, he added hastily: "we may allow ourselves to say that no night had fallen."

Other Whigs, such as Charles Sumner, responded more positively to the Charles River Bridge decision. Sumner was Simon Greenleaf's replacement in the Harvard Law School while the latter appeared in Washington to argue the bridge case in early 1837. Sumner greatly admired Greenleaf, but his adulation of Story bordered on the religious. He had studied with the justice, and their political and legal views generally coincided. But the Charles River Bridge controversy found the two men on opposite sides. Regretfully, Sumner told his mentor that he fully agreed with Greenleaf's arguments and the Warren Bridge cause. After the decision, Sumner acknowledged the force and power of Story's dissent but refused to view the majority decision as the apocalypse.

The Whig-oriented *Boston Courier* also refused to be frightened by the decision. It dismissed as frivolous the claims of the "vested rights class" that the Court had pronounced "radical and revolutionary doctrines." The *Courier* contended that the only important question was charter construction, and the newspaper left little doubt that it supported Taney's refusal to imply rights not expressly authorized. Finally, the *Courier* had little sympathy for those who feared the worst consequences from the decision. The Court, it insisted, had announced no new doctrine and in no way had authorized an invasion of private property rights.

Democrats could not restrain their enthusiasm for the new "Democratic Court" and its decisions, but surprisingly few went so far as to herald a "revolution" and an overturning of traditional constitutional law. In June 1840, the *United States Magazine and Democratic Review* published a lengthy reply to Chancellor Kent's public assault two years earlier on the Taney Court. The anonymous writer challenged Kent's criticism as wholly political, and demonstrated that the 1837 decisions were supported by Marshall Court opinions and doctrines. He also suggested that the real complaint was not that the Taney Court had overturned or rejected Marshallian doctrine, but rather that it would go no further. He said that the new court had maintained the old decisions, while it refused to "receive *dicta* as judgments, or to make old cases the stepping-stones to new aggressions upon State rights." Thus, for some, there was satisfaction in the consolidation of existing doctrine, the thwarting of further encroaching nationalism, and the restoration of a "proper equilibrium" between the states and the federal government. That kind of change was sufficient.

The idea of a judicial revolution in 1837 presupposes that the Marshall Court left a legacy of clear and cohesive doctrines. But by Marshall's death, sufficient vagueness, ambiguity, and contradiction existed within the total body of his work as to make every man his own Marshallian. Take, for example, the problems presented in the Charles River Bridge case. If Marshall's opinion in the Dartmouth College case is accepted as his last, or his authoritative, statement on public contracts, then the new Chief Justice significantly altered Marshall's doctrine. But Marshall's Dartmouth College opinion, and Story's concurring elaboration, left ample room for the implementation of the strict construction interpretation. If that were not enough, Marshall also delivered the Providence Bank opinion, and concurred in three other contract clause cases that utilized strict construction. Though Taney never mentioned Dartmough College, he adroitly availed himself of the four more recent precedents. Rather than suggesting that Taney overturned Marshall, or that Charles River Bridge constituted a judicial revolution, it is more proper to recognize that Taney was a faithful practitioner of *stare decisis*—a role into which he very carefully cast both himself and his colleagues.

Focal perspectives largely determined the immediate reaction to the Charles River Bridge case and to the other key decisions of 1837. Daniel Webster, who could predict nearly every Marshall Court decision and its reasoning, was understandably shaken by rulings which undermined so many of his articles of faith. Democratic spokesmen, on the other hand, who for decades had railed against centralizing opinions of the Supreme Court—the last Federalist bastion—now saw their cherished views of state rights and powers apparently endorsed by the high tribunal. Such opinions accurately reflected the immediate results of the decisions. The outcome certainly shocked those who believed that the old bridge proprietors really had a vested property right, that New York's regulations affecting incoming passengers interfered with interstate and foreign commerce, and that Kentucky's state bank corporation was only a blind for the sovereign state's issue of bank notes. But these decisions notwithstanding, private property after 1837 was not subject to expropriation, state police power did not proscribe the steady growth of federal power to regulate interstate commerce, and the states ultimately did not exercise the dominant role in the circulation of money. So what exactly was the meaning of the 1837 decisions?

The constitutional decisions of the first Taney term primarily represented a response to particular issues in a particular time and place. So did the Marshall Court's decisions. They did not signify a retreat from the broad, expansive doctrines of Marshall and his colleagues. Indeed, there remained the same abiding concern for the rights of property and for the authority of government, but with a significant difference in emphasis. Charles River Bridge, and the other cases, indicated the Taney Court's heightened awareness of the social responsibilities attached to private property and similarly the power of government to cope with pressing problems and needs. True enough, the Democratic-dominated court emphasized the role of the state as opposed to the national government. But the existing problems of transportation, communication, immigration, money supply, and others, then were essentially local ones; furthermore, it is questionable whether the national government had the ability — it certainly had not the inclination — to deal with these issues.

The 1837 decisions marked a judicial recognition of industrial and social problems that only local governments could handle. The national political mood, largely dictated by the negative attitude toward national power by the dominant Democratic party, simply rejected vigorous federal power in most areas. Recent and still-present concerns over the tariff, internal improvements, central banking, and slavery, revitalized longstanding prejudices against any positive thrust for the national government. Still, a general antistatism did not prevail. People demanded positive action from government to stimulate and release productive energy, and to protect them from adversity. Thus government — and political circumstances dictated that it be state government — was intimately involved in a variety of endeavors and enterprises. Government built or aided the construction of canals and railroads, expanded educational opportunities, and acted on a wide front of social concerns such as public health, bankruptcy, regulation of the professions, women's rights, liquor, and imprisonment for debt.

In this sense, it is misleading to view the Taney Court within the abstraction of "states' rights." Certainly the judges' views mostly harmonized with the dominant political attitudes toward national power. To some degree, their decisions admittedly enhanced the powers of the states, but not necessarily at any appreciable expense to the national government. The 1837 rulings were power-oriented, and the men of the Taney Court were as vitally concerned as Marshall and his colleagues that government retain its positive protective functions. No less than their predecessors, the Taney Court justices rejected the notions of a weak, dispirited governing force. The theme runs throughout the opinions of 1837. Government exists for the well-being of the community; it must, therefore, have the capacity to act in behalf of the safety, prosperity, and happiness of its people with any legislation conducive to those ends. "The continued existence of government would be of no great value, if by implications and presumptions, it was disarmed of the powers necessary to accomplish the ends of its creation." The words are Marshall's in the Providence Bank case; Taney quoted them approvingly in the Charles River Bridge case. The orientation of the Taney Court justices, combined with the practical political realities, forced an emphasis on the role of the states; still, the ultimate purpose was no different from that which had guided John Marshall.

X

THE DOCTRINAL IMPACT:
IMPLEMENTATION
AND LIMITATIONS

THE CHARLES RIVER BRIDGE case had an immediate, positive influence on American law. The legal profession favorably received its basic doctrine of strict construction. For lawyers and judges, Taney's opinion was a rationale for enjoying, in Taney's words, the "improvements which are now adding wealth and property." Taney correctly recognized that liberally construed charters served privilege at the expense of progress. The newly-chartered railroads throughout the United States faced harassment and opposition from such existing property forms as turnpikes and canals, whose proprietors asserted wildly-imagined rights from charters granted decades earlier. The extent of opposition to change by vested interests on the legislative level cannot be measured absolutely, but the record of litigation from the 1830s onward offers ample evidence of the legal resistance to technological change. The Charles River Bridge ruling offered a convenient doctrine to turn aside these challenges in courts, and undoubtedly operated on the political and legislative level to coerce nonlitigated settlements.

But opposition lingered. As late as 1845, Daniel Webster attacked the Charles River Bridge ruling before a Massachusetts legislative committee. He called it a "lamentable" precedent and claimed that the legal profession had no respect for it. Further-more, he confidently expected that pressure from lawyers and judges ultimately would overturn the decision. In a later edition of his widely-respected *Commentaries,* Chancellor Kent continued to register his disagreement with the Charles River Bridge deci-sion but was less optimistic about reversing it. Discussing fran-chises, Kent clung tenaciously to the common law doctrine that charters should be construed to exclude all contiguous competi-tion. He contended all grants implied that government would not interfere, either directly or indirectly, to impair their value. In a footnote, Kent commented on the bridge case at length and admitted that Taney's strict construction doctrine was now the "prevalent principle" in American constitutional law; he rue-fully added, however, that "it is deeply to be regretted."

Webster and Kent perceived an important, but specifically limited change in constitutional law. Actually, the basic tenets of the contract clause of the federal constitution remained intact and vital; indeed, Taney strengthened and expanded them during his tenure. The Chief Justice and his colleagues regularly affirmed traditional doctrines and judicial zeal for the protection of property rights continued undiminished. *Bronson* v. *Kinzie* in 1843, for ex-ample, offered ample evidence that a state's impairment of private contractual obligations was not the exclusive concern of a Marshall or a Story. Following the panic of 1837, the Illinois legislature decreed that court-ordered sales of mortgaged property could not be consummated unless there were a bid equal to two-thirds of the appraised value. A subsequent act gave mortgagors the opportunity to redeem foreclosures at the purchase price plus ten per cent interest. Significantly, the laws were retroactive. Taney conceded the state's right to alter the remedy involved in the obligation and enforcement of a contract. But by making the laws retroactive, the state had tampered with the contract itself and imposed conditions unknown to the mortgagee at the time of execution. For all his concern with community rights and social realities in the Charles River Bridge case, Taney relied on tradi-tional vested rights views here. His opinion reflected the traditional public policy choice favored by Story in the bridge case, emphasizing security and protection for the risk-taking capital investor. *Bronson* v. *Kinzie* survived until the great depression nearly a century later. In 1934, in *Home Building and Loan Association* v. *Blaisdell,* the Supreme Court frankly recognized the prevailing emergency conditions and allowed the state to alter the remedy for enforcing preexisting debts.

Taney's *Bronson* opinion at last persuaded even his most recalcitrant critics that their fears had been greatly exaggerated. The *Washington Daily National Intelligencer,* a leading Whig organ, now admitted that the Court's decisions had "gone far to dissipate entirely the apprehensions, entertained by some friends of the Constitution, that the character of the Court, as the great balance-wheel of the machinery of this Government, might be injuriously affected by the changes which a few years have brought about in its composition."

#   #   #

The principles of the Charles River Bridge case had their most immediate and widespread impact at the state level. The decision in 1837 came at a most opportune time for state courts that found themselves confronting mounting demands for judicial intervention in questions similar to the Massachusetts bridge imbroglio. In 1828, nearly a decade before the final disposition of Charles River Bridge, the Connecticut case of *Enfield Toll Bridge Co.* v. *Connecticut River Co.* provided a typical example of the judicial dilemma. Saddled with the bonds of vested rights doctrine that Kent and others so glowingly praised, yet sensing the demands for greater flexibility, the Connecticut court sought some means of subordinating existing law to the realities of community needs.

The state had incorporated the Enfield Bridge Company in 1798 to construct a bridge and locks on the Connecticut River, with the right to collect tolls for one hundred years. The charter granted the company exclusive privileges in the area. After completion of the bridge in 1809, the company claimed that it could not construct the locks. The state thereupon relieved the company of its obligation to do so. In 1824 the state chartered the Connecticut River Company to build a canal bypassing the Enfield Falls, thus making the river navigable. The construction was opposite the old locks site. The bridge company thereupon sought an injunction, claiming infringement, but the court denied it because Enfield Bridge had not made a strong enough case for equitable intervention.

The Connecticut court's opinion carefully blended an acknowledgment of traditional rights with a recognition of community needs. First, the court established that the Enfield grant was still valid, including the exclusive rights to a toll bridge and to construct the locks. It found that the legislature had not explicitly discharged the company, but had only suspended its obligation to build the locks. The grant to the Connecticut River Company therefore constituted a diminution of Enfield's exclusive rights. The court cited previous Supreme Court contract clause cases and Chancellor Kent forbidding any infringement of charter rights. To this point the court followed traditional doctrine, including a liberal interpretation of Enfield's corporate rights. But the court refused to issue the injunction on the grounds that it could grant relief only when the party injured was in actual possession. Furthermore, the bridge proprietors were guilty of laches (an undue delay or failure to assert a legal right or privilege) for they had failed to fulfill their obligation.

The court juxtaposed the laches concept with Enfield's vested rights and conceded the importance of the community's needs. "The public have a deep interest in the commodious navigation of *Connecticut* river," the court noted, "and it is peculiarly inequitable, that the rights of a community should be sacrificed, to insure the franchise of the plaintiffs from all possible damage, while they are not in the actual enjoyment of it, and have taken no measures to pay the price of their charter." The plaintiff's failure to benefit or improve the navigation of the river particularly impressed the court.

The Enfield case anticipated Taney's societal concerns in Charles River Bridge. Yet the Connecticut Court found it necessary to conform to traditional vested rights doctrine; only the equally traditional laches doctrine provided the means for circumvention without changing the letter of the law. Thus within the limits of prevailing precedents, the Connecticut court found the means of subjugating vested rights that hampered the development of necessary improvements. But the Enfield case only offered a method for dealing with a special set of circumstances. A broader doctrine was necessary for a frontal assault on the social costs of persistent privilege. Accordingly, the Charles River Bridge case opened the floodgates and courts now directly confronted and denied exaggerated implied claims of vested rights. The state court reports for the next two decades are replete with cases implementing the Charles River Bridge doctrine. Most of these cases involved strict construction and a clear preference for new forms of property or new competition, and at the expense of older property interests.

A New York court endorsed the Charles River Bridge decision within a few months. In *The Mohawk Bridge Co. v. Utica and Schenectady Railroad Co.*, the court refused to enjoin the construction of a railroad bridge adjacent to a chartered toll bridge. The bridge proprietors claimed that their charter prohibited ferry competition and, by implication, any other form of competition. The court, however, insisted upon strict construction and also noted the potential benefits of technological change for the "public good." The bridge's charter, it said, could not deprive future legislatures of the right to provide for the people's needs with an improvement entirely unknown at the time of the grant.

Three years later, the Virginia case of *Tuckahoe Canal Co. v. Tuckahoe and James River Railroad Co.* witnessed Taney's specific concern with canal versus railroad competition. The canal company had been chartered in 1827 and finished construction three years later. In 1837, the state chartered the railroad to another group, but only after the canal owners had refused the opportunity. The railroad crossed the canal at several points. The canal company thereupon sought an injunction on grounds that the railroad bridges impeded the use of the canal and its improvement and enlargement. A lower court issued a preliminary decree, and then dissolved it except for a requirement that the bridges be at least six feet above the tow path. The state high court, however, rejected this stipulation, holding that restrictions could not be imposed in the absence of actual damage.

Judge H. St. George Tucker, speaking for the Court of Appeals, maintained that its charter did not grant the canal company exclusive use of the right of way. The legislature, he said, had the power to grant new charters on the same line even though the value of the first charter would be impaired. Discussing Charles River Bridge at length, Tucker contended that granting implied rights would be dangerous to the well-being of the community, for "monopoly is very ingenious in extending its rights and enlarging its pretensions." He was concerned that the canal's claims, if granted, would cause commercial havoc, for it would mean that the railroads running north and south would be prevented from crossing the canals that ran east and west. The judge concluded that any determination of damages was premature since the canals might claim compensation if the railroad bridges actually blocked barge traffic.

The Taney Court occasionally applied the strict construction principle of the Charles River Bridge case, but the justices set severe restrictions on its use. Strict construction was really a two-edged sword. It could be employed, as in the bridge case, to defend the clear interest of the community and the state but, in cases where private parties held expressly granted rights and privileges, strict construction often resulted in a decision antagonistic to the felt public interest. In Charles River Bridge, Chief Justice Taney had carefully pointed out the perimeters of the strict construction doctrine. Public grants and charters, he said, would be strictly interpreted by limiting rights and privileges to express terms, with all doubts resolved in favor of the public. The corollary here, of course, was that rights expressly granted to private interests would be scrupulously enforced and respected by the courts. In short, the constitutional prohibition against impairment of explicit contractual obligations remained in force.

The Taney Court designed the strict construction doctrine primarily to confirm legislative destruction of any alleged privileges that amounted to a monopoly hold on enterprises affecting the public interest. Another line of cases concerned tax exemptions claimed by publicly-chartered corporations. In both areas, the justices carefully maneuvered between the compulsory demands of the contract clause and the dictating realities of the decisional context.

Some cases called for a relatively straightforward implementation of the Charles River Bridge doctrine. The 1850 decision in *Mills v. County of St. Clair*, for example, confirmed the 1837 ruling in all its particulars. The case involved monopoly rights for a family-owned ferry across the Mississippi River. In 1819, the Illinois legislature had granted ferry rights to the family and further provided that no other person thereafter could establish a competing ferry within a one-mile distance. But at the same time, the legislature reserved the right to repeal the monopoly grant if it proved "injurious to the public good." Fourteen years later the state repealed the grant, and in 1839 authorized the county to operate a ferry from a tract of land adjacent to the existing ferry landing. The state offered no compensation to the family. Webster appeared before the Court as counsel for the plaintiffs and mostly reiterated his Charles River Bridge arguments. Except for Justice McLean, Webster's pleas fell on deaf ears and the Court simply employed its 1837 doctrine rejecting any claim for exclusive privilege or compensation.

The Richmond, Fredericksburg, and Potomac R.R. Co. v. The Louisa R.R. Co. in 1851 indicated more clearly the Court's lack of sympathy for monopoly claims. The plaintiff company had secured a charter in 1834, guaranteeing that the state would not establish another railroad along the same right of way for thirty years. But the privilege contained a hedge by the state, that was perhaps inadvertent, but nonetheless important. The prohibition against a competing railroad was framed out of concern that a competing carrier would diminish the Richmond Railroad's passenger traffic. Fourteen years later the state authorized the Louisa Railroad to continue its freight runs from the southwest to Richmond, and then on a parallel line with the first carrier to Fredericksburg. The Richmond railroad insisted that its grant prohibited the state from authorizing any competitive railroad company. But the Court held that the monopoly privilege applied only to the transportation of passengers, and therefore allowed the state to charter another line for different purposes.

A quarter century after Charles River Bridge, and as Taney's career drew to a close, the Court stretched the strict construction doctrine even further in *Bridge Proprietors* v. *Hoboken Company* (1863). In 1799 New Jersey had granted the plaintiffs a ninety-nine year exclusive privilege to operate a toll bridge over the Hackensack River. Sixty years later the state chartered the Hoboken Company to build a railroad and included in the grant the power of eminent domain to take existing franchises, such as bridges, and to build viaducts and a bridge over the Hackensack River. The company built its bridge, but never sought to condemn the existing franchise. The bridge proprietors then sued, charging a violation of the contract clause. Speaking for the Court, Justice Samuel F. Miller conceded that the original charter was a valid contract. But Miller hastened to add that its construction had to take into account the passage of time and the advance of technology. "In no department of human enterprises have more radical changes been made," Miller wrote, "than in that which relates to the means of transportation." The railroad bridge, he found, was something altogether different from the type of bridge envisioned in 1799; furthermore, its construction did not violate the spirit of the proprietors' charter; their franchise was only an exclusive privilege for a toll bridge.

The New Jersey bridge proprietors' claims had more solid substance than those of the Massachusetts group in 1837 or of the Richmond Railroad. But still the Court found the costs of exclusive privilege intolerable. For what the bridge proprietors wanted in the 1863 case was to build the railroad bridge themselves and thereby exact a tribute from the carrier for passage across the river. Once again, marketplace necessities governed the course of the law. Construction of the bridge by the proprietors would have increased the railroad's operating costs; that in turn might have been passed on to passengers and consumers. This was the kind of constricting and nonproductive privilege Taney anticipated in 1837; now, in 1863, it was specifically rejected by the Court.

From 1837 until Taney's death in 1864, the Supreme Court never overturned a state court decision that applied the Charles River Bridge precedent against explicit claims of exclusive franchise privileges. But in less than a year after the Chief Justice's death, in *The Binghamton Bridge* case, the Court reversed a New York court decision sustaining a legislative charter for a new bridge competitive with an existing franchise claiming exclusivity. The background of the case was remarkably similar to the Charles River situation, although the monopoly claim was more substantial in New York. In 1805, the state chartered the Susquehanna Company with exclusive privileges to build a bridge across the river near Binghamton. Subsequently, the Chenango Company spun off the Susquehanna and, in 1808, the legislature enacted a new authorization for this group to construct the bridge. As the city expanded on both sides of the river, there were repeated efforts to secure a new bridge. But in 1826, and again in 1854, the legislature rejected these applications on the grounds that the proposal impaired vested rights. In 1855, however, the legislature succumbed and incorporated the Binghamton Company to construct a new span. There was really no question of the community's needs. The town had grown substantially and there was evidence that the bridge frequently closed for repairs.

After the new company was chartered in 1855, the Chenango Company applied to the Court of Appeals for an injunction, arguing that their grant gave them a monopoly. The court, however, denied the request on the grounds that the act of 1808, establishing the Chenango Company, did not incorporate the exclusive grant language ("It shall not be lawful for any person or persons to erect any bridge. . . .") of the 1805 charter. But the Supreme Court reversed the decision in 1865. Justice David Davis, speaking for an almost evenly divided bench, contended that he subscribed to the strict construction doctrine of Charles River Bridge, but he insisted that the 1805 charter, with its grant of exclusiveness, was carried along with the legislative changes of 1808. Davis's bow to Charles River Bridge was disingenuous, for his construction of the company's monopoly could only be implied. There was much in Davis's opinion that followed Story, rather than Taney, on public policy and vested rights. Like Story, he brushed aside any consideration of changed conditions and community needs, and insisted upon understanding the proprietors' rights and conditions within the context of their original investment.

Judicial interpretation of alleged grants of immunity from taxation by the state was always a thorny problem. In 1812, in *New Jersey* v. *Wilson*, Chief Justice Marshall had declared that states could, either by charter or by contract, relinquish the right of taxation and that future legislatures could not alter such terms. In his Providence Bank opinion nearly two decades later, Marshall retreated somewhat by holding that the grant of immunity had to be explicit. The Taney Court's commitment to strict construction would seem to have dictated decisions more in the spirit of the Providence Bank case than of *New Jersey* v. *Wilson*. But strict construction was a diffuse and personal thing, and the results were quite irregular and erratic.

Some early cases followed clearly the lines of Providence Bank and Charles River Bridge. For example, in *Armstrong* v. *Treasurer of Athens County* (1842), the Court sustained an Ohio tax on lands formerly held by a state university but subsequently sold to private individuals. The justices agreed that although the university lands had been tax exempt "forever," the benefits did not inure to subsequent purchasers of the property. Similarly in *Philadelphia and Wilmington Railroad* v. *Maryland* (1851) the Court denied tax immunity to a railroad formed out of a merger of several companies, one of which had a tax exemption for its real and personal property. Here the Court applied strict construction as part of a scheme to insure the proper allocation of "necessary public burdens," and refused to extend the exemption to the new company. These decisions clearly utilized strict construction in a practical fashion. The tax exemptions were not specific and expressed;

furthermore, the Court's social and economic cost accounting decreed narrow holdings. But these criteria proved inadequate for maintaining judicial cohesiveness in the Taney Court. The various Ohio bank tax cases in the 1850s highlighted the strains. First, in *Piqua Branch of the State Bank* v. *Knoop* (1851), a majority of the Court held that a state could surrender its sovereign power of taxation. The bank's original charter had provided that the bank would pay the state a fixed percentage of profits; this exempted it from all other taxation. Some years later, the legislature imposed a tax on the bank's stock, claiming that the earlier arrangement only involved a method of taxation and was not a permanent contract. The Court's majority, however, held that there had been a contract and the state's later act had impaired it. The dissenters, largely acting on their interpretation of the implications of Providence Bank and Charles River Bridge, denied that the state ever could barter away its sovereign right of taxation.

The Court completely fragmented in another tax case during the same term, *Ohio Life Insurance and Trust Co.* v. *Debolt.* This time the justices barely sustained an act taxing insurance companies at the same rate as other property, despite a charter provision providing for taxation no different from that levied on banks. Taney probably best summarized the Court's refinement of the strict construction doctrine, reiterating the basic litany, that corporate privileges must be strictly construed against the grantee, and in favor of the public. Furthermore, neither taxation nor any other attribute of sovereignty "which the community have an interest in preserving, undiminished," would be considered surrendered, "unless the intention to surrender is manifested by words too plain to be mistaken." But now Taney added a new dimension to the Court's attitude of restraint toward legislative action. In Charles River Bridge and similar cases, the Court regularly asserted the right of legislatures to act in behalf of the "community interest," with a minimum of judicial interference. In effect, strict construction was the convenient judicial ploy to allow free play to the legislative will. In the *Debolt* case, however, Taney again bowed to the legislature and refused to have the Court judge the wisdom of public policy, even though it might clearly be harmful to the public interest. In other words, even contracts and charters "incautiously made," with "immunities and exemptions from public burdens improvidently granted," would be sustained so long as the privileges were expressly granted and did not violate state constitutional requirements.

During the next decade, the Court used Taney's *Debolt* position in six more Ohio bank tax cases. In each the Court found explicit corporate privileges and ruled that subsequent acts impaired existing contracts. *Dodge* v. *Woolsey* (1855), the leading case in this series, best reflected the nuances of strict construction doctrine. An 1845 act provided that certain banks would pay the state a percentage of profits in lieu of taxes. But the new Ohio constitution in 1851 required uniform corporate taxation and accordingly, in 1852, the legislature changed its 1845 law. The Court's majority held that the 1845 law was constitutional when passed, and despite the community desire, as expressed in the new constitution, any change in the banks' privilege violated the contract clause of the federal constitution. Taney formed part of the majority in each of these cases, but as long as they sat on the bench the three other southerners maintained that legislatures could alter privileges and that new state constitutions could repudiate any prior grants of exemption or immunity. In so doing, they in effect affirmed a doctrine, not merely of state sovereignty, for such is consistent with a dual delegation of sovereign power, and thus with federalism, but rather denied the federal nature of the union, and the clear superiority of explicit federal governmental powers over the powers of individual state governments. Or, in other words, they espoused an extreme form of state rights rejected even by Calhoun.

The problem of tax immunities was related to the broader problem of monopoly privileges. Taney's statements in the *Debolt* case confirmed his 1833 Attorney General's opinion in the New Jersey Camden & Amboy case. He had argued then that monopoly grants could be valid only if expressly conferred by state legislatures. The basic theory of Taney's 1833 opinion implied that legislatures could not bind their successors unless specifically authorized by their constitutions. But the state courts sustained monopoly grants, clearly and expressly granted, in the 1830s and 1840s, and this before the Supreme Court's tax immunity cases.

While state decisions approved monopoly privileges, the courts recognized their frequently stunting and pernicious effects. The implementation of the eminent domain doctrine offered an equitable resolution of the dilemma, providing some compensation for vested rights while freeing the community to develop alternative property forms as needed. Three years before the Charles River Bridge case, for example, the New Hampshire court found valid an exclusive grant for a bridge across the Piscataqua River, but added that the legislature could authorize another bridge upon payment of compensation (*Piscataqua Bridge* v. *New-Hampshire Bridge*, 1834). In *Enfield Toll Bridge Company* v. *Hartford and New Haven Railroad* (1846), the bridge company sought an injunction against the construction of a railroad bridge across the Connecticut River at a point where it claimed exclusive privileges. The railroad had acted under a state law authorizing it to construct needed improvements and granting it the power of eminent domain. Although the Connecticut court acknowledged the validity of the plaintiff's monopoly grant, it held that there was no impairment when the state utilized eminent domain to destroy a property right.

Finally, in *West River Bridge* v. *Dix* (1848), the Supreme Court clarified its position on eminent domain. In Charles River Bridge, Taney had insisted that the non-exclusivity of the proprietors' charter made unnecessary any consideration of their claims to compensation. But in the West River Bridge case, the Court sustained the broad authority of eminent domain, decisively rejecting Webster's arguments that the contract clause restricted its use. The plaintiffs in the case had been granted exclusive privileges in 1795 to construct a bridge over the West River in Vermont and to collect tolls for one hundred years. In 1839, the state authorized local communities to exercise eminent domain over any existing franchise if the "public good" required a public highway. It evidently designed the law to deal specifically with corporate privileges which had been expressly granted. Speaking for the Court, Justice Daniel held that the power of eminent domain was "paramount to all private rights vested under the government," and that such a law did not impair the obligation of a contract.

Thus by mid-century the courts had worked out a position that could at once serve the community's needs and recognize the claims of private interests. Corporate privileges would not be implied; indeed, charters were to be construed strictly and in behalf of the community. But privileges expressly granted, and not prohibited by state constitutions, would be recognized as valid and could be abrogated only by the sovereign power of eminent domain, and with the payment of compensation. The lesson was clear to innovative capitalists. As with the Massachusetts railroad charters of the 1830s, they secured legislative grants which clearly spelled out their rights and privileges. Notwithstanding the demands of investors, states retained the power to destroy property rights and forms in behalf of community progress and need, but at the cost of compensating property owners with fair value.

# # #

Prior to the Dartmouth College ruling, legislatures recognized the wisdom and security of reserving the power to amend, alter, or repeal charters. After 1819, such a clause regularly found its way into state constitutions, general statutes, or individually-granted charters. But legislative exercise of this power encountered evergrowing judicial scrutiny and resistance. Ironically, the judicial technique for restricting legislative power was also strict construction—this time, of the reserved power. Strict interpretations of charters in cases similar to Charles River Bridge constituted judicial restraint, indeed almost a self-abnegation of power in deference to legislatures. But the reserved power cases, being directed against legislatures, led to a bold assertion, and in time, an innovative use, of judicial power. In these cases, there would be one of the important seeds of the substantive due process of law doctrine that was to become in the later nineteenth and earlier twentieth centuries the basic constitutional limitation on legislative power in the United States.

Judicial disposition of corporate litigation involving reserved charter powers did not conform to any neat pattern of doctrine or behavior. The results varied from state to state and were usually dictated according to the factual circumstances of particular cases. Judges sustained the implementation of the reserved power in a broad array of cases involving the safety, efficiency, and operations of private corporations. The Vermont and New York courts, for example, approved legislative requirements that railroads erect cattle guards; Massachusetts and Illinois upheld a wide variety of railroad safety measures for highway crossings and the operation of equipment; the Minnesota high court sustained the legislature's alteration of the route of an exclusive ferry franchise; in approving the consolidation of two railroads, the Connecticut court held that under the reserved power, it was not necessary to secure consent of the stockholders or the directors; and in a series of cases, the New York courts upheld the imposition of individual shareholders' liability for corporate debts.

In many of the cases before the Civil War, the courts manifested a great deal of tolerance of legislative activities involving the reserved power. Much of this reflected prevailing notions of legislative sovereignty and judicial insecurity in the face of rising demands for more direct political control of judges. But courts did strike out against some legislative tampering with corporate charters. Most importantly, judges frequently asserted that their state consitutions required their intervention to insure due process of law.

The beginnings of this development came in 1805 in the North Carolina case of *Trustees of the University* v. *Foy*. The state constitution had established a public university, and to this end, the legislature incorporated the University of North Carolina, granting it all property escheated before or thereafter to the state. A later legislature repealed the generous grant, but the state high court found that this act violated the "law of the land," or due process of law, clause of the state constitution. The judges held that the clause restricted legislative power from depriving corporations, as well as individuals, of their property rights. Ten years later, in the United States Supreme Court case of *Terrett* v. *Taylor,* Justice Story distinguished corporations as public or private bodies, and discussed the degree of legislative control over each, holding that judicial action must accompany any attempt to destroy or resume a private franchise. Private corporations, he said, could lose their franchises by a misuser or nonuser of them; such franchises could be resumed by the government upon a *quo warranto* proceeding and a judicial judgment to ascertain the forfeiture. Story further invoked the dictates of natural law in order to deny that legislatures could repeal statutes creating private corporations or divest such corporations of their property without their consent or default. In this, Story said, he stood "upon the principles of natural justice, upon the fundamental laws of every free government, upon the spirit and letter of the constitution of the United States, and upon the decisions of most respectable judicial tribunals, in resisting such a doctrine."

State court judges periodically affirmed Story's views. By 1832, the Maryland court confidently asserted the "well known" rule that forfeiture of a charter for misuser or nonuser could only be enforced by judicial proceedings. In this case, *Chesapeake and Ohio Canal Co.* v. *Baltimore and Ohio Railroad Co.,* the court held that a corporation may be dissolved by legislative enactment, with the consent of the corporation, but added that "such forfeiture must be judicially ascertained and declared upon direct proceedings against the corporation for that purpose, in order that it might not be condemned unheard, for an imputed delinquency." The court carved out its role carefully, insisting that the forfeiture be enforced by a writ of *quo warranto* or *scire facias.* The Maryland court said that government must obtain forfeiture "by judicial action, and not by legislation." Charles River Bridge had no effect on this aspect of legislative-corporate relationships; in 1839, in *Planter's Bank of Prince George's County* v. *Bank of Alexandria,* the Maryland court re-affirmed its position.

In these cases, courts had acted upon vague natural law principles or ancient common law concepts. But in the 1830s, judges turned to the strict construction of the reserved power to limit legislative attempts to destroy or alter corporate charters. Justice Story again led the way. In the circuit court case of *Allen* v. *McKean* (1833), Story struck down an attempt by the Maine legislature to reorganize the governing structure of Bowdoin College. The state constitution specifically prohibited state aid to any literary institution unless the state retained the power to alter, limit, or restrain the powers vested in the institution. Originally, the college had been chartered by Massachusetts, but after the Act of Separation in 1819, it agreed to put itself under the reserved powers of the new state of Maine. In 1821 the Maine legislature passed a series of laws affecting the tenure of Bowdoin's president and the composition of the board of trustees. President Allen sued the school treasurer for payment of his salary for the period following his removal as president. Story held in favor of Allen for a variety of reasons. Most importantly, he narrowly interpreted the reserved power clause of the constitution and in the college's agreement with the state by contending that the clauses permitted only changes beneficial to the institution. In 1854 the Kentucky high court followed Story's version of the reserved power and added that the power to alter or amend the charter of a theological institute could be carried out only with the consent of the trustees *(Sage* v. *Dillard)*.

In these years, courts increasingly found implied limitations upon reserved powers. For example, in *Miller* v. *New York and Erie R. R.* (1856), a New York court virtually turned Charles River Bridge on its head, holding the ambiguity of the reserved power against the state. The case involved a railroad charter that contained a reservation clause. Some two decades after incorporation, the state had enacted a law requiring the railroad to construct roads across its tracks at its own expense. The court found the statute void on the grounds that it constituted the taking of private property without compensation. Again, a court sustained Story's doctrine of beneficiality in *Allen* v. *McKean*. "It would be preposterous to say," the court found, "that the legislature has the power to make any and every requisition upon the defendants as a condition of their retaining their corporate existence." Once the court concluded that the state's act amounted to the taking of property without compensation, the reserved power was irrelevant; the power of taking without compensation could not be reserved, "for none such could have existed." Chief Justice Lemuel Shaw in Massachusetts three years later expressed similar views (*Commonwealth* v. *Essex Co.*).

The Supreme Court invoked the contract clause of the federal constitution as a limitation on the reserved power in a number of cases. In *Curran* v. *Arkansas* (1853), for example, the Court repudiated a state's direct claim that its reserved power could abridge the rights of creditors and impair the obligation of contracts. Arkansas had enacted an amendment to the charter of a state-owned bank that freed the bank's assets from creditor claims. The state court sustained the amendment, but on appeal, the Supreme Court reversed. For the Court, Justice Benjamin R. Curtis totally denied the state's assumption that it could impair, alter, or destroy the existing contract between the bank and its creditors, without properly repealing the charter. Curtis did not say that outright repeal would also have impaired the contract, but his opinion, along with several others in these years, indicated that the Court would not have tolerated such unilateral action by the legislature.

The drive for judicial superintendence of legislative alterations of corporate powers was neither consistent nor uniform. Indeed, there was an equally significant amount of judicial obeisance to the legislative will. Justice Marcus Morton of the Massachusetts high court reflected the thinking of the "Jacksonian Judge" on this as well as on the considerations of the Charles River Bridge case. In *Crease* v. *Babcock* (1839), Morton practically gave the legislature *carte blanche* to alter or amend charters, specifically rejecting a plea that the power to declare a charter forfeited was exclusively judicial. Without saying whether legislative acts were conclusive in all situations, Morton held that the reserved power was ample to work a forfeiture in this case. Perhaps the leading example of blanket judicial approval of legislative power came from an Iowa territorial court in *Miners' Bank* v. *United States* (1848). The court sustained a legislative repeal of a bank charter, eschewing any examination of legislative motivation or inquiry into the facts. "However oppressive it may appear for a party to contract to reserve the right of rescinding the same at pleasure," the court noted, the state's power to do so was unquestionable. The court also expressed an unusual amount of tolerance for legislative wisdom and impartiality, saying that legislators "act in a judiciary capacity, and are not amenable to the odium attached to a party who reserves the right of being a judge in his own case."

The conflict over absolute legislative power came to a head with the Pennsylvania legislature's sordid actions involving railroad charters in the 1850s. These occurred during the intense struggle between Philadelphia and Baltimore for commercial supremacy and the routes to Pittsburgh and beyond to Ohio. The legislature, responding to the influence and manipulation of Philadelphia interests, and acting under a reserved power, repealed the charter of the Erie and North East Railroad in 1855. The Pennsylvania Supreme Court subsequently denied the railroad's plea for an injunction restraining the state from taking over the line *(Erie and North East R. R.* v. *Casey,* 1856). Justice Jeremiah S. Black, whose views were quite similar to Morton's, and who had written a number of opinions resisting corporate attempts to inhibit legislative action with the law of the land doctrine, upheld the legislature's repeal of the railroad charter. Black contended that if the original charter contained a repeal clause, the exercise thereof was not an impairment of contractual obligation, but rather an enforcement of it. Furthermore, Black disavowed judicial intervention. Legislatures, he said, were the sole judges of misuser, and despite the railroad's correction of the abuse for which it had been cited, the state had the right to repeal the charter once the wrong was done, and no compensation had to be paid.

Chief Justice William Lewis delivered a biting dissent, presaging familiar judicial language of later years. The lack of due process in the state's dealings with the railroad shocked Lewis, and he also sharply disagreed that the facts of the case justified repeal of the charter. Lewis conceded that legislatures could repeal charters when corporations engaged in illegal or fraudulent activities, but he maintained that the issue must then be adjudicated since the validity of the act depended upon the existence of facts that only a jury could determine. Lewis completely accepted the plaintiff's arguments that the repeal constituted a deprivation of property without judgment of its peers and thus contrary to the law of the land. The stockholders, Lewis concluded, had the right "to demand that their property shall not be taken away unless ... by due course of law as administered by the constitutional tribunals where alone the judicial power is vested."

The railroad rivalry flared up again in the Pennsylvania Legislature in 1864 when the Pennsylvania Railroad lobbyists secured repeal of the charters of two small western railroads, both closely allied with the Baltimore and Ohio Railroad. By now, however, some legislators realized the potentialities of judicial intervention and warned that vested rights could not be abrogated in a summary fashion. "No court in the country will sustain our repeal," warned one legislator, while another insisted that "the Legislature cannot take away a corporate franchise without reference to the courts as to the forfeiture." This time, the railroad bondholders brought their suit into the federal courts, and in a circuit court opinion in 1865, Justice Grier made prophets of the minority legislators. Jeremiah Black, now retired from the state court, appeared as a lawyer defending the repeal. Black emphasized his own opinion in the Erie case of 1856, but Grier tersely rejected the argument, and adding insult to injury, asserted that the governing principles of law were best stated by Chief Justice Lewis's Erie dissent. In short, Grier fully accepted the view that the question of misuse or abuse of a charter was a matter for judicial determination.

While the bondholders appealed in federal court, they also instituted *quo warranto* proceedings in state tribunals, but the trials and appeals extended for several years until 1868 when the state supreme court granted a final decree in favor of the aggrieved railroads. Times and political forces had changed; and the legislature unanimously moved to repeal the repealer. Legislators apparently conceded the field to the judiciary. One senator flatly maintained that the earlier repeal assumed judicial functions that violated the separation of powers principle. Again, there was reference to the due process-law of the land concept; as the senator noted, unless the legislature respected "not only the law of the land, but the universal God-like law of right and justice, there can be no justification for refusing to restore to this corporation the charter of which it was deprived by a violation of those principles, revered throughout the world wherever civilization has penetrated."

The lesson was clear. Judicial intervention was a latent but potent device for restricting capricious legislative abuses of charter and franchise rights. For the rest of the century relatively little litigation resulted from the exercise of reserved powers. That power was used, as illustrated for example in a study of lumber and stream-use franchises in Wisconsin. But the paucity of litigation there indicates that the charter repeals and alterations generally had the consent of the grantees, and that they were beneficial. When not, courts stood willing and able to protect franchise holders whose rights were violated.

#   #   #

Although both state and federal judiciaries had declined Daniel Webster's invitation to substitute their judgment for the legislature's in the Charles River Bridge case, American courts did not abandon their vigilance in behalf of vested rights claims. The Charles River Bridge decision had its uses, of course, particularly in order to sustain desirable changes beneficial to the larger community but thwarted by obstructionist, outmoded interests. It served to strike down a variety of claims to vested title, and courts usually used it against exaggerated or inert claims barring vital material and technological improvements. But it certainly had no levelling effects. Thomas Cooley, the foremost legal commentator of the late nineteenth century, was as devoted as Webster, Story, and Kent to the protection of property and the enforcement of contract. Three decades after the Charles River Bridge decision, however, he considered its strict construction principle as well-settled; furthermore, he maintained that it was "sound doctrine," that ought to be "vigilantly observed and enforced." Cooley's judgment and advice have been followed continuously as the principles of the case have been used to accommodate the vast flow of technological innovation and change in the same spirit as when Taney cleared the legal obstacles to railroad development at the expense of existing interests.

XI

⌒

PRIVILEGE
AND CREATIVE
DESTRUCTION

THE CHARLES RIVER BRIDGE case confirmed an evolving shift in the legal standing of vested privilege. Whatever the validity or merit of their claims, politically the Charles River Bridge proprietors never could refute the charges that their claims to exclusive privileges constituted an intolerable stranglehold over the community. But this charge, albeit politically effective in Massachusetts, was not the basis of their loss in court. Legally, they floundered on the strict construction of their charter, and nothing else. Certainly Massachusetts Chief Justice Parker was right when he suggested that no such assault would have been made on the proprietors in the years just following the completion of the bridge. By the 1820s, however, the risks and the technical feats involved in building the bridge were all but forgotten and submerged by ever-increasing community resentment.

The Charles River Bridge proprietors were victims of the popular outburst against privilege that was part of the fashionable political rhetoric of the times. This of course was not a levelling attack, and it was scarcely motivated by an animus against property, or even against wealth. Attention was directed rather toward interests entrenched and prospering through special privileges that had been gained through acknowledged legal means. Further-more, there was a link drawn between privileged status and socially unproductive property. Property represented power, but it was also the vehicle for advancing the material well-being and happi-ness of the community. Jacksonian rhetoric emphasized the need for balance and therefore directed its greatest invective against the wealthy, powerful, and established interests that sought to exclude competition. Property was no blessing to society when it represented what Theodore Sedgwick called "ill-gotten, *dispropor-tioned* wealth, . . . obtained by unfair dealings, by fraud, by oppres-sion, by monopoly, by which I mean *legal privileges given to some, and denied to others.*" The Second Bank of the United States was the na-tional symbol of "ill-gotten, disproportioned wealth"; in their local setting, the Charles River Bridge proprietors were similarly stigmatized.

Yet this was only an argument of convenience, suited to temporal and spatial considerations. The Charles River Bridge was a mag-nificent achievement, and one warmly received, in the eighteenth century communities of Boston and Charlestown. But during the next century—with population growth and economic expansion—the bridge symbolized an oppressive monopoly, imposed upon the communities because of special legal privileges obtained, as some charged, by unfair dealings and fraud. The five year legislative fight waged by the free bridge advocates, alternating rationaliza-tions of need with attacks upon privilege, was a brilliant lobbying effort. But it did not permanently alter legislative policies. For while the legislature destroyed the proprietors' pretensions to exclusive privileges, they shortly thereafter granted specific monopoly rights to railroad investors. To some extent, the bridge affair had alerted potential railroad investors to the need for some protection against future legislative caprice, and thus they insisted upon specific exclusivity for their right of way. Although legis-lators had made monpoly grants limited in time, they had to barter privilege for a desirable public good. Compared to the Charles River Bridge charter of 1785, the Boston and Worcester Railroad charter of 1831 represented a higher form of privilege. The

legislature granted the railroad a thirty year monopoly on its right
of way and authorized the railroad directors to establish such rates
of tolls as they deemed fit. The bridge proprietors, on the other
hand, were obligated to follow a precisely detailed schedule of
tolls. In some ways the Charles River Bridge controversy cost the
community dearly. Private investors demanded and secured a
Chinese Wall of protection around corporate rights. The quest for
entrepreneurial liberty, which began as a drive for opportunity as
against vested privilege, culminated in new privileges, protecting
newly-gained opportunities and ventures.

The Massachusetts railroad situation was not unique. Privilege
or public subsidy is generally a necessary component of any public
policy that has to rely on private initiative for economic goals. The
question of its use is not easy. The problem is a distributive one;
that is, how to so apportion and limit privilege as to serve the immediate needs of the community, yet prevent it from becoming an
undue or lingering burden, exacting an unjust reward or stifling
new developments potentially more beneficial to the community.
In his classic *Report on Manufactures* in 1791, Alexander Hamilton
set down a guiding policy by suggesting that there was "no purpose
to which public money can be more beneficially applied than to the
acquisition of a new and useful branch of industry." Public aid and
privileges for new undertakings were, Hamilton said, "justifiable"
and "oftentimes necessary"; yet he warned that continuance of aid
for products or services long established, "must almost always be of
questionable policy."

Grants of privilege take various forms. Patents and copyrights
for exclusive exploitation are classic examples of governmental
encouragement; the aim of these is to promote the well-being of
both the innovator and the society. But public policy privileges are
often more direct, such as, for example, outright subsidies, tax
immunities, and other privileged exemptions involving tenure,
charges, or special powers like eminent domain. The federal government today offers a direct subsidy and preferred position to the
American merchant marine; it underwrites the operating costs of
airlines by building and maintaining airports and guidance sys-

tems; the well-known oil depletion allowance ostensibly encourages the exploration and drilling of new oil fields; railroad charters of the nineteenth century commonly provided for the exercise of eminent domain by the carriers in order to facilitate their right of way; and, of course, the 1785 charter for the Charles River Bridge offered the proprietors the inducement of a forty year tenure with the right to collect tolls. The public policy thrust and purpose in each case facilitated the development or maintenance of certain services deemed vital to community interests without involving government as the exclusive operator. Although popular preference demanded private initiative and enterprise, the hazards of risk, the physical obstacles, or the immense outlays of capital generally forced governments to assist the formation of public services through some form of privilege. It is difficult to imagine the existing national air transportation system being created and operated without direct governmental assistance. Similarly, the Charles River Bridge promoters would probably not have committed themselves to the financial and physical risks of the bridge without the guaranteed tenure and right to collect tolls.

Properly apportioned, privilege has beneficial uses. While often secured through vigorous, intensive lobbying, a grant of privilege in the United States is openly-gained and granted as a specific expression of desirable public policy. Certainly American legislative history is not free from fraud or criminal manipulation, such as bribery. But privilege or favor gained in this manner is ephemeral and easily nullified in the courts or at the ballot box. In short, privilege is accepted, even condoned (perhaps too readily) to stimulate or maintain investment, and with certain restrictions, it is available to any entrepreneurs or interests whose need can be justified to public policymakers.

Yet when privilege lingers beyond the point of community need, and becomes a source of profit primarily to the holder, it becomes a burden and may retard further innovations. The persistence of certain privileges in the French economy of the *ancien régime* offers a case in point. There, for example, the multiplication of internal tolls and tariffs covering the means of transportation and communication hampered the growth of a national common market. The tolls generaly accrued to a parasitical nobility that had secured exclusive rights from the state decades and sometimes centuries before. Domestic producers, such as iron manufacturers, had to pay numerous internal duties to secure raw materials and to ship their goods; meanwhile, foreign competitors were often exempt. Consequently, French products grew more expensive the farther the goods travelled from the manufacturing site; this limited both the marketability and the flow of domestically produced items. Such a situation hardly served the public policy goals of either the advocates of mercantilism or those of laissez faire. But they were fully enmeshed in and supported by a legal and customary system until the upheavals of the French Revolution.

The record of public policy in the United States regarding grants of privilege offers a direct contrast to the French experience.* Most legislative policymakers in the United States have operated with a conscious regard for maintaining a balance between private groups and the interest of the larger community. From the very beginnings of the American republic, legislative bodies were alert to the dangers of persistent privilege. Influenced chiefly by the anti-monopoly rhetoric and actions against British commercial policies prior to the American Revolution, legislators carefully prescribed grants of economic privilege. They granted privileges in recognition of the value and usefulness of particular ventures, but with a perception that privilege ultimately outlives its purpose and becomes burdensome to the community's well-being. Various restrictions developed on privileges, such as time limits in the original gift and prospective rights of revocation or regulation. Indeed, the history of public

---

*In a circular letter of October 1, 1832, signed by a number of leading Charlestown figures including Robert Rantoul, a prominent legislative leader in the free bridge fight, the continuance of tolls on the Warren Bridge was attacked and compared to European experiences: "[T]o imitate the arbitrary practice of many nations in the old world, of deriving a revenue from taxes on internal intercourse, would be impolitic, unjust, and anti-republican; . . . ANTI-REPUBLICAN, because introducing among us one of the most odious of those interferences with the freedom of the people which make despotism every where hateful." Rantoul Papers, Essex Institute Library.

policy has been marked by a reserved governmental right to regulate or prescribe activities as a *quid pro quo* in exchange for some form of privilege.

But statutory limitations, either as to tenure or to supervision, were inadequate to the task of protecting society against some of the pernicious effects of privilege. They could not, for example, take into account the onrush of technological change, which in a constantly evolving process, pressures old forms of property with newer ones. In this context, the problem has been one of accommodating and absorbing desirable and needed change in opposition to existing privileged interest. The doctrine of the Charles River Bridge case provided, and continues to offer, the formal answer because it fashioned a legal doctrine to justify the process of creative destruction—a continuous process whereby new inventions and enterprises create new goods and services, and to destroy existing ones, all under the often empty banner of progress, improvement, and need.

The Charles River Bridge case provided the legal rationale for endorsing and promoting creative destruction. It is this aspect of the case that transcends the relatively limited conflict over bridges in the Boston area, making it a landmark involving the interrelationship of public policy, technological change, capital developments, competition, and law. These larger considerations occurred throughout the case. In his arguments on behalf of the Warren Bridge before the state supreme court in 1829, Richard Fletcher contended that the principles of "liberal competition" as opposed to the claims of vested privilege were at stake in the case. Improvements and new inventions, he said, promoted progress. Fletcher recognized that their implementation could injure or destroy existing forms but maintained that the larger social and community advantages outweighed individual privations. State Supreme Court Justice Morton also offered his judicial blessings. He feared that a liberal construction of privilege would amount to a stipulation that communications, business, and the state of the society and the nation, "remain stationary." Morton, too, conceded the damaging consequences of innovation, but he rejected the alternative consequences of economic stagnation that accompany an unreasonable extension of privilege.

Chief Justice Taney's Supreme Court opinion clinched the point. For him, the Charles River Bridge case offered a convenient opportunity to create a legal covering for public policy choices favoring technological innovation and economic change at the expense of some vested interests. In line with prevailing ideology, Taney stressed what Stuart Bruchey has labeled "corporate egalitarianism," whereby the community promotes and sanctions competition and new enterprise for its own well-being. Indeed, the Chief Justice's most telling contribution was his perception of the long-range implications of the basic issues in the Charles River Bridge case. As Taney noted, to concede the proprietors' claims would have threatened a moratorium on the adoption of innovations that offered potentially injurious competition to existing enterprises or services.

In 1837, the nation was on the threshold of dramatic changes in communications and transportation. Although the railroad was in its infancy and was still some distance from realizing its full potential, it offered obvious advantages and convenience over existing canal and turnpike services. Capital investments in railroads proceeded apace, and the web of lines developed to link production and markets on a larger and more efficient scale than ever before. Railroad grants naturally paralleled or overlapped existing routes, whether turnpike or canal. The operators of those passageways usually held grants for exclusive control of the line of travel. But if those claims or titles were so interpreted as to exclude alternative and potentially more useful forms, such as the railroad, the community and society would be shackled with existing services, and "obligated to stand still," as Taney observed. The people of the community desired, however, "to avail themselves of the lights of modern science, and to partake of the benefit of those improvements which are now adding to the wealth and prosperity, and the convenience and comfort of every other part of the civilized world." The law that Taney and his colleagues laid down in Charles River Bridge accommodated such aspirations, even to the point of condoning either the destruction of or injury to already existing property forms. Vested rights, of course, generally retained their status and preferred position in American law and society; but after the Charles River Bridge case they were more subject to the pressures of public policy considerations which usually favored the advantages of innovation and change over the status quo.

This has been the recurring meaning of the Charles River Bridge case. It immediately served to refute only the more extravagant and vulnerable turnpike and canal claims against the railroads, just as Taney anticipated. But it paralleled developing public policy that allowed creative destruction. In a wide variety of actions, legal decisions have sanctioned injury or destruction, without compensation, to various property forms in behalf of innovative enterprises deemed more desirable and beneficial to the community at large.

But even as courts have followed Charles River Bridge in putting a high social value on creative destruction, they have maintined stable and rigid requirements for eminent domain. Both compensated and uncompensated aspects of regulatory power have reality in American legal history, and courts periodically have been called upon to establish some line of demarcation between the two. Federal and state constitutional principles require that the public pay for private property taken for public use; but the determination of a "taking" often is a slippery proposition. Generally, when government desires economic assets in order to obtain the same yield for the public's interest that the private owner would secure from them for his own gain, the public must pay. Furthermore, if public policy deprives the private owner of all opportunity to use his assets for his own purposes, again compensation must be paid. But when government neither uses private assets, nor makes it impossible for the owner to enjoy them for his own gain, then there is no "taking" in a legal sense, even though the private interest might be harmed by the governmental action.

Decisions sustaining the relocation of old highways and construction of new roads at the expense of existing facilities offer a prime example of the operation of creative destruction. Highway development is a constantly evolving process, involving new, more efficient routes. Individuals and enterprises serving highway traffic, such as gasoline stations, motels, and restaurants, are subject to the risk of administrative actions that may completely alter their competitive standing. For example, a decision to build a new superhighway some miles distant from an existing road, or to convert a road into a limited access highway, often destroys the desirability of a business location.

The state courts almost without exception have supported such decisions, maintaining that property owners and businessmen have no vested right in any route. The courts explicitly have recognized the fantastic economic costs to the community if they granted compensation to such individuals when governmental action destroyed their livelihoods. For example, a Texas court has not only held that the costs of such compensation would be prohibitive, but has emphasized that primary consideration must be given to community needs. "The highways ... are for the benefit of the travelling public, and are only incidentally for the benefit of those who are engaged in business along its way." Those who develop service enterprises along the right of way must recognize, the court said, that new roads might be developed that will divert travel (*State Highway Commission* v. *Humphreys, et al.*, 1933). The California Supreme Court specifically recognized that compensation or concern for existing facilities would result in an "embargo" upon the creation of needed roads (*People* v. *Granni*, 1933).

As in the Charles River Bridge case, the diversion of travel has been sustained under the broad authority of the police power, without consideration to eminent domain. The results can be quite brutal. In Wisconsin, an individual opened an automobile repair shop and gasoline station adjacent to a state road in 1951. The following year the state converted the road into a controlled access highway, but the proprietor still had two driveways leading to the thoroughfare. In 1959 the state highway commission announced its intention to limit access further, with the result that the business was now located over two miles from the nearest interchange. The proprietor sued the commission for damages equal to the loss of business. But the state supreme court held that the public could not tolerate "changeless roads in a changing society." It sustained the state's right to design roads in the interest of public safety and convenience, and without regard or consideration for access to the plaintiff's business. The court held that the public's need and interest in a convenient and efficient national road system was greater than the individual's right to maintain his place of business (*Stefan Auto Body* v. *State Highway Commission,* 1963). Occasionally, as was true in this case, an isolated jurist will argue that where the closing of direct access destroys a man's livelihood, the action constitutes a taking of property and the individual is entitled to compensation. But judicial cost accounting rarely includes such liabilities for the state and the public.

In the modern American economy, similar choices have been made by the various quasi-legislative and quasi-judicial regulatory agencies of the federal government. The decisions of the Civil Aeronautics Board offer particularly useful and relevant examples of the governmental and legal role in abetting creative destruction. In 1938 Congress charged the CAB with the responsibility of developing and regulating air transportation in the United States. Significant technological advances in design had by that time measurably increased the cruising range, speed, and general capabilities of aircraft. In addition, airport and terminal facilities had been expanded and numerous airlines were in a position to capture from the railroads a large share of intercity passenger travel. The war intervened, but only temporarily delayed the inevitable choice. Acting under its statutory authority to develop air transportation, the CAB during the postwar years consciously pursued a policy of promoting and favoring airlines at the specific expense of the railroads. Many circumstances have contributed to the decline of railroad passenger service, including state and local taxing policies, railroad labor, the loss of mail traffic contracts, and, of course, willful neglect by the carriers themselves. But the public policy of an inherently antagonistic governmental agency perhaps has had the greatest impact in diverting patronage from trains to airplanes.

The *New York-Florida Case* of 1956 exemplifies the CAB's basic position. After protracted hearings, the Board awarded Northeast Airlines a new route for the New York to Miami run. After discussing their selection of Northeast and dismissing the severity of the impact on the other air carriers, the CAB turned to the contention of the railroads that it must assess the effect of expanded air service upon surface carriers operating between the same points. The Board offered them little comfort, however, holding that even if the railroads could submit evidence that air competition was destructive, their position would be rejected. The Board was not, it said, "required to consider ordinary competitive impact upon the railroads as a public interest factor, and certainly not to the extent of identifying and treating ordinary diversion from railroads separately." Furthermore, the CAB held that it would not "retard air transportation for the railroads' protection and benefit"—in brief, existing services would not be protected from competition; instead, it would promote new innovations and improvements, even at the expense of the old. Finally, the Board noted that the Civil Aeronautics Act of 1938 commanded it to develop and preserve the advantages of air transport. The CAB usually relied upon this language to shun any consideration of whether the impact of its decisions upon other carriers affected the national interest. But in the *New York-Florida Case*, the CAB argued that a loss of revenue to air competition by surface carriers was not adverse to the public interest. If anything, the Board concluded, the presumption should be to the contrary: for air traffic was more in accord with the national interest because it provided superior service—"fast, dependable, and safe."

Governmental promotion of innovations even extends to a vigilance against attempts by the existing, established services to capture control of the new. For example, in 1958 the CAB denied the application of the Railway Express Agency to operate as an international airfreight forwarder *(Railway Express Agency Inc. Airfreight Forwarder Application)*. Section 408 of the aeronautics act stipulated that the air transport system be free of control by surface carriers. The purpose of that provision, as interpreted by the CAB, is to enable the Board to determine whether a particular control relationship is consistent with the public interest, especially if it involves the independence of air carriers from other competitive services. The railroads controlled Railway Express and could therefore lower its air freight costs by using rail facilities for the domestic part of shipment. The Board also noted that the REA had transportation agreements with ocean carriers. As such, the CAB had considerable doubt that the REA was a proper medium for promoting air competition against the ocean carriers.

The CAB's investigation of airline discounts for military personnel in 1959 illustrates a more direct governmental role in promoting destructive competition *(Certified Air Carrier Military-Tender Investigation)*. Shortly after the airlines instituted military discounts, the railroads protested to the CAB, despite a similar policy of their own. The Board sustained the air carriers' action; it held that without the discount the airlines would not have been able to break the railroads' near-monopoly of transporting military personnel. Curiously, the CAB's examiner had found that the airlines' 10 percent military discount constituted unlawful discrimination against other passengers. But the Board evinced more concern with the air carriers' competitive position *vis-à-vis* the railroads', and it approved continuance of the discount so that the airlines could "enjoy a fair share" of the military travel market.

The decisions of the Federal Power Commission approving the expansion of natural gas service illustrates even more vividly the policy of promoting alleged improvements in behalf of the community while disregarding totally the operations of existing services. A united front of coal mine operators, the coal miners' union, and the railroads regularly opposed applications for the introduction of natural gas in the 1930s and 1940s. But like the CAB, the Federal Power Commission generally refused to assess the impact of a newly developed service upon existing enterprises. For example, in considering the application of gas pipeline and gas service companies to introduce natural gas in North Dakota, the FPC rejected the pleas of intervenors, saying that its authority did not extend to weighing the broad social and economic effects of the use of various fuels *(Kansas Pipeline & Gas Company and North Dakota*

Consumers Gas Company, 1939). In various similar cases, the Commission insisted that it would place primary emphasis on consumer demands for cleaner and more efficient fuels. It conceded that the introduction of natural gas would often cause a significant loss of business to coal companies. But the FPC maintained that such evidence could not be determinative "where considerations of the broad public interest—the interest of all potential consumers, the public welfare, or national defense—outweigh the adverse effect that natural gas service might have on competitive fuels." *(Commonwealth Natural Gas Corp., et al,* 1950)

The FPC's position on consequential damages is analogous to the Charles River Bridge doctrine. Given its quasi-legislative role, and its responsibility for promoting and regulating diverse sources of power, the Commission has insisted that it does not completely disregard competing economic interests. But that consideration has apparently never been determinative, for the FPC repeatedly has held that merely showing adverse economic results to a competing interest would not bar approval of applications for new gas service. Economic consequences to existing operations, particularly coal, have had no effect on the FPC's conscious desire to promote the natural gas industry *(Transcontinental Gas Pipe Line,* 1957).

# # #

Chief Justice Taney's Charles River Bridge opinion struck a vital note for the future of public policy in the United States. His evaluation of the tension between existing, vested interests and innovations and new property forms led him to a resolution of the conflict through emphasis on community needs and rights, insofar as legal realities allowed. The issue has persisted to the present day—as has Taney's disposition of it.

Governmental policy, of course, has not consistently encouraged competition and, in fact, has protected certain interests. Yet technological innovations considered desirable (because allegedly beneficial to the community) have been stimulated and fostered by government, with little sympathy expended on existing interests. While often unrealized in actual practice, competition remains a key value in the legal system's relation to economic policy. The Antitrust Division of the Justice Department and the courts retain a keen interest in enforcing the antitrust laws, although their efforts are often diluted by bureaucratic inertia or frustrated by political hostility within the government itself. In tort law, bona fide competition is a privileged defense, and any economic detriment must be shown to include malice. The Fourteenth Amendment's protection of property rights, the Supreme Court has said, does not protect a business against competition. State courts have held that incompetence, understood as an inability to match competition, is neither a defense nor a cause for action.

The process of creative destruction, and its place in public policy, often has had a salutary effect on American economic development. Yet Taney's concern in the Charles River Bridge case for the reception of technological innovation beneficial to the community is deceptively simple: if applied indiscriminately, his doctrine would identify change as an absolute good. The concept of creative destruction, in application, has been tinged by motives of greed and blighted by deleterious side-effects. Benefits accruing to the larger community are often purchased at the expense of individual losses and injuries, and the costs can be high. Sometimes the long-range costs make creative destruction on behalf of presumed community interests a bad bargain, even by the goals of the policymakers. The promotion of air travel to the point of virtually obliterating rail service has been of questionable value, and now we find policymakers searching for a more desirable mix of transportation forms. Governmental policy alone, of course, has not been responsible for the decline of railroad passenger traffic. Nor can any administrative commission be singled out as responsible for any perceived malformations of transportation policy. Every agency focuses almost exclusively on its subject of interest, with little regard to related services. Consequently, there is virtually no coordination or comprehensive planning and there is, therefore, no agency trying to serve large, national needs. Then, too, divergent policies of Congress and the Executive contribute further to the confusion of aims. Much the same can be said for other areas of governmental concern, such as power and energy needs, communications, health, and environmental control.

Innovative technology often operates now in a mindless market characterized by the breakdown of the classic system of existing demand. The explosion of technology has generated its own creative force, imposing new, often premature, goods and services upon a society without a pressing need for them. The acceptance of innovation sometimes results from political pressure, or a bureaucracy's advancement of its own vested interests, with little consideration of actual need or of possible harmful side-effects. The promotion of the supersonic transport by the Federal Aviation Agency and influential congressmen is a striking example. Final presidential approval rested on the nebulous consideration of national prestige, and this overrode issues of economic need, public and private costs, feasibility, noise levels, airport runway and terminal congestion, and atmospheric pollution.

As Taney observed in the Charles River Bridge case, the choices can be difficult. The visualized benefits of change may have only short-run effects, while the accompanying destruction of existing institutions or services can be totally debilitating and irretrievable. The changes can be unnecessarily disruptive and can contribute to a distortion or deflection of larger goals. But in a nation that puts a premium on the release of creative energy, and views progress as an end in itself, such careful social and economic cost accounting is the exception and not the rule. The dilemma of formulating policies that will allow people "to acquire the things they covet and which will not debar them from the peaceful enjoyment of those possessions which they have already acquired" — as Tocqueville characterized it — is the same as that which confronted legislators and judges in the Charles River Bridge imbroglio in the nineteenth century. The Supreme Court's decision offered a seemingly practical resolution. The law promulgated by Taney was no exercise in abstraction; it was a synthesis, however imperfect, of principle and, more prominently, of expediency. It reflected, and it has continued to serve, the innovative and acquisitive values of the American people.

But the other side of the case, as represented by Justice Story's dissenting opinion, casts a shadow on that synthesis. Taney's principles confirmed and enhanced basic and useful ideas of positive government, but the facts of the case did not entirely support either his legal doctrines or his noble purposes. In the Charles River Bridge case, the accommodation of innovation, which so concerned Taney, did not correlate with the models he himself projected. The Chief Justice spoke of obsolete property forms that thwarted the community's need for improvements and progress; but the legislative decision to create a new bridge was not a technological advance. Instead, the purpose was to relieve the community of tolls — a purpose possible of accomplishment only by taking the existing bridge. Unwilling to implement eminent domain, the legislature followed a less expensive, but somewhat disingenuous, course. In effect, the result was that the legislature infringed on the proprietors' site value, and denied them all practical use of their situation by destroying their opportunity to collect tolls for the life of the bridge's charter. For Story, the state's action constituted a taking that entitled the proprietors to compensation. Taney never confronted Story's challenge; his use of the strict construction doctrine technically relieved him of any responsibility for discussing eminent domain.

History unfortunately obscures dissenters whose views are not ultimately vindicated. But transcending this particular case, Story's objection offers a persistent and always relevant challenge to government's ever-present potential for arbitrariness and insensitivity. The losers' stakes in the Charles River Bridge case were relatively small, limited to a handful of speculative stock shares. In a modern, complex, and interdependent economy, however, public policy choices are more abrasive to larger numbers of individuals and interests. Innovations can carry losses and irreparable harm in their wake, and the choices we make cannot always be dictated by an optimistic estimate of the greater good of the greater number. Progress exacts a price, and ideally, its costs ought to be distributed according to a delicately balanced concept of the public interest.

Surely, it is not always just — or even useful — to rescue that interest from the altar of privilege, only to sacrifice it in a holocaust to immediate popularity.

NOTE:

JOHN MARSHALL AND THE CHARLES RIVER BRIDGE CASE

IN EACH of the three great constitutional decisions of the Taney Court's first term—the Charles River Bridge Case, *New York* v. *Miln,* and *Briscoe* v. *Bank of Kentucky*—Justice Joseph Story dissented at length from the opinion of the court. His dissents were characterized by laments for the "old law," and with a view of himself as standing fast against the tide of revolutionary change. The Charles River Bridge decision was particularly painful for Story. After the first arguments in 1831, he had prepared an opinion favoring the old bridge proprietors, yet he never persuaded a majority of the Court. He carefully designed his opinion to meet the divergent views of his colleagues, but given the rapid changes in the Court's composition, it survived, largely unaltered, only as a dissent.

Historians have readily assumed that Chief Justice John Marshall supported Story's position in 1831. Discussing Story's abortive attempt to carry the Court in 1831–1832, Charles Warren concluded: "It seems that, as the Court stood in 1832, Story, Marshall, and Thompson were in favor of reversing the decree of the Massachusetts Court."[1] Although Warren hedged slightly, his judgment

[1] *The Supreme Court in United States History,* 2:233 n. Warren was not the first to state that Marshall had concurred with Story; his analysis, however, has been cited most often and authoritatively.

has been widely followed. Considering Marshall's views of vested
rights, and the fact that the Chief Justice and Story seldom disagreed on major constitutional questions, Warren's statement, and
its general acceptance, seems natural and logical. Yet there is no
direct evidence to sustain such an interpretation, and indications
are that Marshall and his close friend differed with each other in
the Charles River Bridge case.

The Marshall Court first heard the bridge case arguments in
March 1831, with Justice Gabriel Duvall absent because of his wife's
illness. Besides the Chief Justice and Story, present were Justices
William Johnson, Smith Thompson, John McLean, and Henry
Baldwin. There is no known account of the proceedings of the
Court's conference. But either at the direction of his colleagues, or,
what seems more likely, on his own initiative, Story prepared a
draft opinion in November 1831, favoring the claims of the Charles
River Bridge proprietors. A month later Story sent a copy to
Jeremiah Mason, but he admitted that the justices were divided on
the issues. Apologizing for the length of his opinion, Story told
Mason that he had designed it "in the hope of meeting the doubts
of some of the brethren, which are various and apply to different
aspects of the case." Furthermore, he expected "to gain allies" with
his elaborate defense of liberal construction of franchise charters.[2]

But by March 1832, Story was less optimistic. Writing to Mason
again, Story reported that the case remained undecided. Justice
Johnson had been absent the entire term because of illness; as for
the other judges, they remained according to Story, "greatly divided in opinion and it is not certain what the finale will be."[3] At
the same time, the *Washington National Intelligencer* reported that
the case would be continued because of differences among the
judges.[4] Unfortunately, neither Story nor any other contemporary
source provided a breakdown of all the judges' individual positions.

The Court's Minutes of March 3, 1832 recorded the diversity of
opinion, the lack of a full court, and raised the possibility of new

---

[2] G. S. Hillard, *Memoir and Correspondence of Jeremiah Mason,* 336-37.
[3] W. W. Story, *Life and Letters of Joseph Story,* 2:91.
[4] March 14, 1832.

arguments. In February 1833, counsel for the Charles River Bridge proprietors moved for reargument, and it was so ordered.[5] Absences, deaths, resignations, and vacancies, however, intervened and the case drifted until a largely reconstituted bench assembled for the January 1837 term. The call for new arguments in February 1833 indicated real doubts and uncertainty within the Court. But judicial absences forced further postponement. Subsequently, Justice Johnson died in August 1834 after a lengthy illness and, a few months later, Duvall resigned. With two vacancies, the Court was at an impasse, at least for the Charles River Bridge case. Even before the Chief Justice's passing in 1835, it was clear that the Marshall Court would never decide the issues. Story's opportunity to affirm his cherished "old law," if it existed at all, was only a fleeting one.

The Court's Minutes and calendar, the justices' physical condition at the time, and some of their expressed views, offer some clues into a fairly complex division. Certain votes can be easily discovered. Story's earlier draft opinion and his 1837 dissent clearly put him on the side of the plaintiffs. Thompson concurred in Story's published opinion and it is a fair assumption that his position, too, was constant throughout. Justice Baldwin sided with the defendants in 1837, though he later published a separate statement in which he claimed that he alone among the Marshall Court justices opposed the claims of the Charles River Bridge proprietors.[6] McLean, as indicated in his separate 1837 opinion, consistently argued that the Court had no jurisdiction in the case. In all probability McLean also favored the proprietors' claims on the merits of the case in 1831, as he did six years later. Duvall's absence during arguments probably did not deter him from participation in the decision-making process. The Marylander was deaf and oral arguments obviously had no impact on him. Even if Duvall joined in the

---

[5] Webster reported that Johnson and McLean opposed a second argument. Webster to Dutton, January 29, 1833. Webster Papers, Dartmouth College Library.

[6] Baldwin's statement was not altogether clear. Writing in 1837, he said: "[I]t now appears that I stood alone after the argument in 1831." Baldwin, *A General View of the Origin and Nature of the Constitution and Government of the United States*, 2.

conference deliberations, his position cannot be clearly delineated. Duvall seldom spoke for the Court during his more than two decades on the bench. He probably supported Story's traditional views. But two important earlier constitutional cases point up the difficulty of determining Duvall's vote. In 1827 he joined Marshall and Story in *Ogden* v. *Saunders,* the only major constitutional case in which the Chief Justice felt compelled to disagree publicly with his colleagues. But in the Dartmouth College case a few years earlier, without opinion, Duvall dissented from Marshall's landmark decision.[7] In any event, whether Duvall supported Story, Baldwin, or McLean, or whether he abstained altogether, Story's opinion did not have majority support. At a minimum, there were two votes (Story's and Thompson's) definitely in favor of the old bridge proprietors; even with Duvall on his side, Story still fell one vote short of carrying the Court. Accordingly, the positions of Marshall and Johnson are crucial for understanding the full extent of the division and the Court's subsequent failure to decide the issue. If both had agreed with Story and Thompson, there would have been a clear majority, regardless of Duvall's participation. If Duvall supported the plaintiffs, then either Marshall or Johnson disagreed with Story. So it is certain that one or both joined McLean or Baldwin, despite the latter's claim that he was the only justice to support the Warren Bridge defendants. We only can speculate on the possibilities.

Johnson's position is vague, and it is likely that he never revealed any certain views to his colleagues. He was present during the original arguments in March 1831. It is unknown whether the justices discussed or formally voted on the case that spring. But later that year, and during the first months of 1832, while Story was circulating his draft opinion, Johnson was ill and absent the entire time. Johnson's historical reputation as a maverick on the Marshall Court (albeit somewhat exaggerated) makes him a likely candidate for opposing Story's traditional position. But Johnson's contract

[7] In 1833, Webster was confident of Duvall's support, believing him "generally sound, on such subjects." Webster to Dutton, January 29, 1833. Webster Papers, Dartmouth College Library.

clause views, with the exception of his votes in the bankruptcy cases of *Sturges* v. *Crowninshield* and *Ogden* v. *Saunders,* generally conformed to those of his colleagues. Indeed, in *Fletcher* v. *Peck,* he relied more on a natural law-vested rights position with regard to impairment of contracts than did the Chief Justice himself. Altogether there is little concrete evidence for determining Johnson's position in Charles River Bridge. It is a good guess that he never disclosed or indicated a final conclusion.

Marshall's position, and the available evidence regarding it, raises the most intriguing possibilities. The fact that Story wrote a draft opinion for the Charles River Bridge case might indicate that Marshall opposed or was undecided about the proprietors' cause. Throughout his long tenure the Chief Justice regularly served as the Court's spokesman in important constitutional decisions. But Marshall's ability to lead had declined sharply in his last years. His own failing health, the Court's changing membership, and numerous absences combined to force a deadlock in a number of important suits. It is possible, of course, that Marshall did not regard the Charles River Bridge case of such importance as to require his writing the Court's opinion. Furthermore, he may have been preoccupied with the Cherokee Nation case that was argued at the same time. Yet when Story sent his draft to Mason in November 1831, he mentioned that the case raised "so important a constitutional question," that he was anxious to have Mason's advice and counsel to buttress his own arguments.

The best evidence for suggesting the possibility that Marshall favored the Warren Bridge defendants is only indirect and hearsay. Like Sherlock Holmes's observation about the "curious incident of the dog in the night-time," Story's silence about Marshall's role offers in this case a valuable clue. In his dissenting opinions in *New York* v. *Miln* and *Briscoe* v. *Bank of Kentucky,* Story unhesitatingly invoked the support of his departed leader, specifically citing the Chief Justice's views in those cases. In *Miln,* Story offered lavish tributes to Marshall's previous commerce clause opinions and contended that the new Court's decision blatantly violated wise precedents. Story maintained that New York City's argument had been

emphatically rejected by Marshall when first offered by counsel in
Gibbons v. *Ogden*. At the end of his dissenting opinion in 1837, Story
noted Marshall's participation in an earlier hearing of the *Miln*
case, and concluded: "I have the consolation to know that [in the
previous hearing] I had the entire concurrence, . . . of that great
constitutional jurist, the late Mr. Chief Justice Marshall."[8] In his
Briscoe dissent, Story similarly stated that a majority of the sitting
justices, including Marshall, had found the Kentucky bank act unconstitutional after it was first argued before the Court.[9]

Story was probably more physically and emotionally involved in
Charles River Bridge than the other 1837 cases. His lengthy efforts
in the controversy, and his numerous comments about it in his correspondence, graphically illustrate the importance he attached to
the case. If Marshall, "that great constitutional jurist," had in any
way expressed or hinted sympathy for the plaintiffs' cause, certainly Story would have invoked his spectral support. Other than
acknowledging that differences existed among the justices after the
first Charles River Bridge hearing, Story never referred to Marshall's position at any point in his 1837 dissent. With the exception
of justifying jurisdiction in answer to McLean, and of brief allu-
sions to the general principles for the protection of property rights
in *Fletcher* v. *Peck,* Story avoided any citations to Marshall's opinions
in support of his own arguments. Most significantly, Story never
discussed Marshall's Providence Bank opinion, which Taney had so
deliberately exploited. And how ironic that Story watched Taney
justify the new bridge charter by relying upon a Marshall opinion
while he could not counter with the Master's sayings.

In contrast to his statements in the other decisions, Story's complete silence concerning Marshall in the course of his sixty page dissent is striking and perhaps indicative of the possibility that the two
men differed in the Charles River Bridge case. They were not
necessarily in complete disagreement, of course. Marshall could
have conceivably supported McLean's jurisdictional position, or he
simply might not have formulated any definitive conclusion at all.

[8] 11 Peters 161.
[9] 11 Peters 328.

Either posture would have justified Baldwin's later claim that he stood alone in behalf of the defendants after the 1831 arguments.

The final bit of evidence is only hearsay and comes secondhand from Simon Greenleaf, the leading counsel for the Warren Bridge proprietors in the 1837 hearings. Greenleaf was the American editor of a prominent English treatise on property. Commenting on the Charles River Bridge case in an 1850 edition of that work, Greenleaf claimed that he was "credibly informed that he [Marshall] held the charter of Warren Bridge constitutional, upon the first argument of the case; and that it was on account of [the] division of the bench that a second argument was ordered, which he did not live to hear."[10]

Greenleaf was a cautious man, held in the highest esteem by his contemporaries. Certainly he would have been anxious to invoke Marshall's name in support of his own arguments, and the information was somewhat self-serving. But a number of people who had participated in the case from its beginnings were still alive, among them Justice McLean and Daniel Webster, and it is hard to believe that a man of Greenleaf's reputation and character would have published a story that others, perhaps better informed, could easily refute. Interestingly, Chancellor Kent's son included the story in a later edition of his father's *Commentaries*.[11] Greenleaf was in a good position to be "credibly informed," as he put it. He could have heard the information from what he regarded as a reliable source during his stay in Washington while arguing the Charles River Bridge case in January 1837. Furthermore, he was very friendly with Justice Story, who could have been his informant. Or Story might have told Charles Sumner, Greenleaf's replacement at Harvard during his absence, and he in turn may have divulged the story to Greenleaf.

In any event, Story's silence on Marshall's position in his opinion and correspondence, taken together with Greenleaf's statement, casts substantial doubts on any simple conclusion that Marshall

[10] Greenleaf's, *Cruise*, 3:68.
[11] 7*th* ed., 3:566-67.

favored the Charles River Bridge proprietors. In addition, the Providence Bank case of 1830 points up Marshall's acceptance of the strict construction doctrine. Admittedly, the facts and implications of the case were somewhat different from those in Charles River Bridge. By the Rhode Island law, taxation diminished bank profits, but not to the point of destruction, which was what Massachusetts in effect did to the old bridge's tolls when it chartered the Warren Bridge. Could Marshall have tolerated such capricious violation of the spirit of the Charles River Bridge charter as to lead to confiscation of the proprietors' property? If we interpret Marshall's concern for property rights merely as an abstraction exclusively preoccupied with the protection of titles, it is difficult to imagine that he could have approved the Massachusetts legislature's action of 1828. But Marshall's great line of contract clause opinions from *Fletcher* v. *Peck* on consistently touched on the relevance of property rights to larger considerations of political economy. The essential message always involved a premium on ventures, and a recognition of their broad socio-economic benefits, rather than on holdings per se.[12] In the Charles River Bridge case, if Marshall perceived the same inhibiting effects of liberal charter construction on mercantile development as Taney and Morton, then, the Chief Justice, however reluctantly, could have supported the state's action. Chances are that he did.

[12] See, in general, Chapter V, *supra*.

BIBLIOGRAPHICAL ESSAY

CENTRAL TO MY understanding and interpretation of the Charles River Bridge case are the writings of Willard Hurst. The "release of enèrgy" theme is described in his seminal work, *Law and the Conditions of Freedom in Nineteenth Century America* (Madison, 1956). This idea, and others useful for the study of legal history, are in his *Law and Social Process in United States History* (Ann Arbor, 1960) and *Law and Economic Growth: The Legal History of the Lumber Industry in Wisconsin* (Cambridge, 1964). I derived the corollary theme of "creative destruction" from Joseph Schumpeter's *Capitalism, Socialism, and Democracy,* 3rd ed. (London, 1950). A fresh reading of Alexis de Tocqueville's *Democracy in America* (Vintage ed., New York, 1954) always provides pertinent insights into American society and character during the nineteenth century.

There is a lengthy account of the case in Charles Warren, *History of the Harvard Law School* (New York, 1908), Vol. I. Warren discusses the case in his *The Supreme Court in United States History* (Boston, 1922), Vol. 2, in the context of transition from the Marshall to the Taney Court. The most complete discussion of the case's place and importance in constitutional law doctrine is in Benjamin F. Wright, *The Contract Clause of the Constitution* (Cambridge, 1938). Louis Boudin, *Government by Judiciary*, 2 vols. (New York, 1932) and in his "John Marshall and Roger B. Taney," 24 *Georgetown Law Journal* 864 (1936), treats the case as an important episode in the development of American capitalism. Other works that offer some broader understanding are Wallace Mendelson, *Capitalism, Democracy, and the Supreme Court* (New York, 1960), ch. 3; Henry Graff, "The Charles River Bridge Case," in John Garratty (ed.), *Quarrels That Have Shaped the Constitution* (New York, 1966); and Charles G. Haines and Foster H. Sherwood, *The Role of the Supreme Court in American Government and Politics, 1835-1864* (Berkeley, 1957). The larger problem of public policy and economic development is treated with extensive examples in E. M. Dodd, *American Business Corporations Until 1860* (Cambridge, 1954); John W. Cadman, *The Corporation in New Jersey* (Cambridge, 1949); Louis Hartz, *Economic Policy and Democratic Thought: Pennsylvania, 1776-1860* (Cambridge, 1948); and Oscar and Mary Handlin, *Commonwealth: A Study of the Role of Government in the American Economy* (New York, 1947). The biographies of Supreme Court justices of the period vary in the extent of their treatment. Basic of course is Carl Brent Swisher, *Roger B. Taney* (New York, 1935) which, despite certain shortcomings, stands as the best biography of Taney. It is important for its resurrection of Taney from being a discredited servant of the "Slave Power" as a result of his Dred Scott opinion in 1857. Gerald T. Dunne's *Joseph Story* (New York, 1971), superbly fills an important need.

I developed the local story of the Charles River and Warren Bridges from public records and pamphlet literature. The official actions are summarized in the United States Supreme Court's printed record, now available in the National Archives. I supplemented this with *Records, Massachusetts Bay Colony* and *The Laws of Massachusetts*. Although sponsored by the Charles River Bridge proprietors, the *Review of the Case of the Free Bridge Between Boston and Charlestown* . . . . (Boston, 1827) includes a complete record of the petitions and arguments of both sides. Also valuable were *The Commonwealth's Interest in the Bridges and Other Avenues into the City of Boston,* Report by Attorney General to the Senate, January

19, 1835; *Report Relating to Warren and Charles River Bridges,* Joint Report of State Senate and House Committees, February 1836; and *Charles River Bridge Report,* April 2, 1836. These are available in Massachusetts Legislative Documents. David Henshaw's anonymously published pamphlet, *An Appeal to the Good Sense of the Legislature and the Community in favor of a New Bridge to South Boston* (Boston, 1825) reflects the spirit and demands of the free bridge forces while Lemuel Shaw's, *Reasons, Principally of a Public Nature Against a New Bridge from Charlestown to Boston* (Boston, 1825) demonstrates the constitutional and policy considerations of the proprietors and their supporters. Frederick L. Oliver, "The Bridges over the Charles," *Bostonian Society Proceedings* (1952) details the engineering and statistical data of the bridges. I found a summary of Harvard's financial connection with the Charles River Bridge in the University's General Catalogue, 1944. Relevant Harvard records from the University Archives are available in a special collection in the Treasure Room of the Harvard Law Library.

Caleb H. Snow, *A History of Boston* . . . . (Boston, 1825) covers the concerns of the Boston town government. Arthur Darling, *Political Changes in Massachusetts, 1824-1828* (New Haven, 1925), can be used, but with some caution, for the political implications of the free bridge controversy. Stephen Salsbury, *The State, the Investor, and the Railroad: The Boston & Albany, 1825-1867* (Cambridge, 1967) is excellent for economic and public policy impact. Levi Lincoln's correspondence in the Massachusetts Historical Society provided some insight into the pressures exerted upon him. The Boston newspapers, such as *The American Traveller,* the *Columbian Centinel,* the *Independent Chronicle and Boston Patriot,* the *Courier,* and the *New England Palladium and Commercial Advertizer* offered detailed reporting of legislative affairs, 1823-1837.

The state court arguments and opinions are in 6 Pickering 376 and 7 Pickering 344 of the Massachusetts Reports. Additional materials for this aspect of the case are in the published Supreme Court record and the various newspapers mentioned above. Daniel Webster's connection with the case throughout its various hearings is discussed in Maurice Baxter's *Daniel Webster and the Supreme Court* (Amherst, 1966). In addition, I used some important Webster papers at Dartmouth College. Leonard W. Levy's, *The Law of the Commonwealth and Chief Justice Shaw* (Cambridge, 1957) also was helpful. Simon Greenleaf was an important figure in American law during the middle of the 19th century; unfortunately there is no adequate study of his varied legal career as attorney, court reporter, teacher, and scholar. His manuscript notes portray the heat and passion of the 1837 arguments better than the printed record. They are with the Charles River Bridge collection in the Harvard Law Library. Justice Henry Baldwin published a separate, rather idiosyncratic opinion for the Charles River Bridge case, as well as the other important ones in the 1837 term, in *A General View of the Origin and Nature of the Constitution and Government of the United States* (Philadelphia, 1837).

The petitions and memorials of 1836–1837 are in the published legislative materials; in particular, see Senate Documents No. 24 (January 1836) and No. 83 (April 1836). Some of the flavor of the dogged fight by Charlestown interests to remove the tolls in the 1830s can be found in the Robert Rantoul Papers, Essex Institute Library. For example, Benjamin Crowninshield wrote to Rantoul, a state legislator, on October 13, 1832: "Nothing can be more impolitic than these obstructions to transportation as these turnpikes and bridges, sucking, like parasitical plants, over the body of a territory, sap its energies, and the whole community feels the withering effect of their silent and insidious influence."

The Charles River Bridge decision did not arouse much comment outside Massachusetts. The *Miln* and *Briscoe* cases appeared more significant at the time and attracted more attention. But Chancellor Kent wrote a scathing attack on Taney's opinion in *The New York Review* (April 1838), 2:372–404. An anonymous response, probably written by Charles Ingersoll, appeared in the partisan *United States Magazine and Democratic Review* (June 1840), 7:497–515. Critical, but more balanced, was Charles S. Davies' essay in the *North American Review* (January 1838), 46:125–156. Important insights for the transition between the Marshall and

Taney Courts can be found in R. Kent Newmyer, *The Supreme Court Under Marshall and Taney* (New York, 1968) and Gerald Garvey, "The Constitutional Revolution of 1837 and the Myth of Marshall's Monolith," *Western Political Quarterly* (March 1965).

My basic insight into French differences on privilege concepts derived from several lectures on French economic history and some articles by Paul Bamford of the University of Minnesota. Also helpful were John F. Bosher, *The Single Duty Project* (London, 1964) and Francois Crouzet, "Croissances comparées de l'Angleterre et de la France au XVIIIᵉ Siècle," *Annales, économies, sociétiés, civilisations* (1966), 254–291. The literature on problems of eminent domain is quite vast. Particularly useful for shaping my thinking were Frank I. Michelman, "Property, Utility, and Fairness: Comments on the Ethical Foundations of 'Just Compensation' Law," 80 *Harvard Law Review* 1165, and Joseph L. Sax, "Takings and the Police Power," 74 *Yale Law Journal* 36. Hurst's *Law and Economic Growth* and Howard J. Graham, *Everyman's Constitution* (Madison, 1968), ch. 10, were helpful on the limitations of the reserved power. Finally, for problems of the impact of technological change upon the economy and society, see *Technology and the American Economy*, Report of the National Commission on Technology, Automation, and Economic Progress, Vol. I (February 1966); House Committee on Science and Astronautics, Subcommittee on Science, Research, and Development, *Technology Assessment*, 90th Cong., 1st Sess. (Washington, 1967); and a most perceptive and disturbing essay by Arlen J. Large, "Technology in the Mindless Market," *Wall Street Journal*, October 17, 1969.

ACKNOWLEDGMENTS

The usual amenities for services rendered apply in spades in my case. Of course I convey only gratitude, not responsibility. My largest debt undoubtedly extends to Willard Hurst, Vilas Professor of Law at the University of Wisconsin. His criticisms and insights constantly enlarged my perspective. Paul K. Conkin, Harold M. Hyman, Alan D. Harper, and Morton Rothstein clarified my ideas and my writing—with what I can only describe as brutal generosity. Some of my graduate students offered significant research aid and served as sounding-boards for my ideas. In particular, I must mention George Parkinson, William Wiecek, Andrew King, Daniel Madden, Janet Kortens, and David Allen. The Russell Sage Foundation and the American Council of Learned Societies provided fellowships for a most profitable year in the University of Wisconsin Law School with a Residency in Law and Social Science.

My wife, Sandy, and my children, Jeff, David, Susan Anne and Andy, contributed enough to justify putting their names in print.

S.I.K.

December, 1970
Madison, Wisconsin

INDEX

Hamilton, Alexander, 157
Hancock, John, 11
Harvard College, 6-8, 10, 18, 32, 74, 76-77, 80, 87-88, 111, 114
Henshaw, David, 16, 21-22, 29
Home Building and Loan Association v. *Blaisdell* (290 U.S. 398 [1934]), 135
Hughes, Charles Evans, 89
Hurst, Willard, 67

Independent Chronicle and Boston Patriot, 112
Injunction proceedings, 3, 36-41

Jackson, Andrew, 54, 56, 58-61, 72, 75, 84
Jarvis, William C., 29
Jefferson, Thomas, 55, 60, 62, 70, 119
Jerome and others v. *Ross* (7 Johnson's Ch. 315 [N.Y., 1823]), 39n
Johnson, William, 55, 57, 173-175 *passim*
Jones, Walter, 57
Judiciary Act of 1789, 45n
Judiciary Act of 1801, 119
Judiciary Act of 1837, 119

Kansas Pipeline & Gas Company and North Dakota Consumers Gas Company (2 FPC 29 [1939]), 166-167
Kent, James, 25, 37, 39n, 70-72, 117-120, 129, 134, 136, 153, 178

Laches, 136-137
Law of the land. See due process of law
Leggett, William, 58, 60, 121
Lewis, William, 151-152
Lincoln, Levi, 22, 27-29, 32-33
Locke, John, 68
Lowell Journal, 33, 34

McLean, John, 56, 57, 59, 61, 84, 96, 126, 139, 173-175, 177-178
Madison, James, 54, 55
Malden Bridge, 13

Marbury v. *Madison* (1 Cranch 137 [1803]), 60
Marshall, John, 3, 20, 21, 54-61, 64-69, 71-72, 81, 85, 86, 119-120, 122-132, 134, 142, 172-179
Martineau, Harriet, 96
Mason, Jeremiah, 173, 176
Massachusetts Constitution, 25, 36, 37, 42
Massachusetts legislature, 1, 2, 4, 6-15 *passim,* 18-34 *passim*
Massachusetts Supreme Judicial Court, 2, 35-53, 62-63
Middlesex Canal, 19, 23, 51
Middlesex County, 9, 13, 15, 28, 29, 51
Miller, Samuel F., 140
Miller v. *New York and Erie R. R.* (21 Barbour 513 [N.Y., 1856]), 149-150
Mills v. *County of St. Clair* (8 Howard 569 [1850]), 139
Miners' Bank v. *United States* (1 Greene 553 [Iowa, 1848]), 150-151
Mohawk Bridge Co. v. *Utica and Schenectady R. R.* (6 Paige 554 [N.Y., 1837]), 137
Monopoly, 15-17, 43-44, 51-53, 115, 144-145, 156-157
Monroe, James, 56
Morton, Marcus, 45-47, 50, 52, 83, 113, 150, 151, 160, 179

New Jersey v. *Wilson* (7 Cranch 164 [1812]), 65n, 66, 142
New York American, 60
New York Evening Post, 58
New York-Florida Case (24 CAB 94 [1956]) 165
New York Review, 117
New York v. *Miln* (11 Peters 102 [1837]), 119-120, 124-126, 172-176
Niles, Hezekiah, 58

Ogden v. *Gibbons* (4 Johnson's Ch. 150 [N.Y., 1819]), 39n